Sound Practice

Phonological Awareness
in the Classroom

Lyn Layton, Karen Deeny
and Graham Upton

David Fulton Publishers
London

This book is dedicated to the memory of Grace Buchanan. With Grace's enthusiasm, support and encouragement, the idea for a research project was turned into a reality.

David Fulton Publishers Ltd
Ormond House, 26–27 Boswell Street, London WC1N 3JD

First published in Great Britain by David Fulton Publishers 1997

Reprinted 1998

Note: The right of Lyn Layton, Karen Deeny and Graham Upton to be identified as the authors of this work has been asserted by them in accordance with the Copyright, Designs and Patents Act 1988.

Copyright © Lyn Layton, Karen Deeny and Graham Upton

British Library Cataloguing in Publication Data
A catalogue record for this book is available from the British Library

ISBN 1–85346–456–2

Typeset by Kate Williams, London
Printed in Great Britain by Bell and Bain Ltd, Glasgow

Contents

Acknowledgements

We would like to express our gratitude to the Department for Education and Employment, the Oak Foundation, and the Children's Research Charity for funding the investigation from which this book has grown. We are also indebted to the staff and children in the many schools and pre-school groups, where the fieldwork was carried out: their contributions, both to the investigation and to this book, have been invaluable.

Our thanks are also due to the many people who have provided constructive criticism of draft chapters of this book. These include colleagues in the School of Education at the University of Birmingham. Additionally, we would like to thank the following for their teacher's-eye views: Lynne Elvins, Judith Izzo, Cicely Olive, Phyllis Mott, Anne Rickard and Pauline Westbury.

Illustrations by Loretta Wall.

The Background to the Book

From 1992 to 1996, a study, supervised jointly by the University of Birmingham and Hereford and Worcester Dyslexia Association, investigated the possibility of preventing written language difficulties by training pre-school children in phonological awareness. A key feature of this study, *Phonological Awareness and the Pre-School Child*, which involved over 250 4-year-olds, was the design, implementation and evaluation of a resource pack for the routine targeting of phonological skills in nursery classes.

As researchers engaged on the study we maintained a strong commitment to translating research into everyday classroom practice. Our study has shown that phonological training can be accommodated in nursery settings. Improved phonological skills in young pre-readers are, however, unlikely to be translated into effective reading and spelling strategies unless teaching specifically addresses the role of phonological processes in the development of independent literacy.

Many professionals, some of whom we have worked with collaboratively, and others who have attended our lectures and presentations, have pointed to the need for a text, both to inform teachers about phonological awareness, and to make practical suggestions about how to promote it in the classroom. This book is one response to that need: it is intended to provide practitioners with sufficient knowledge and understanding to enable them to maximise the potential of phonological tasks for all children acquiring literacy.

About the Authors

Lyn Layton is a Research Fellow in the School of Education at the University of Birmingham. She is a qualified teacher of pupils with Specific Learning Difficulties and has taught adults and children with a range of written language problems, including dyslexia, for many years.

Karen Deeny is a practising Speech and Language Therapist with a particular interest in pre-school children with special needs. She has also taught children with specific written language difficulties, and was, until recently, a part-time Research Associate in the School of Education at the University of Birmingham.

Professor Graham Upton is Pro-Vice-Chancellor of the University of Birmingham where he is Professor of Special Education and Educational Psychology. He has taught in ordinary and special schools, and been involved in teacher education for over 20 years. In addition, he has conducted funded research and written widely on many aspects of special education.

Introduction

Twenty-five lively 4-year-olds are excitedly getting ready for a session in the gym. They are peeling off jumpers, struggling out of trousers, kicking shoes aside. The nursery teacher surveys the scene, and suggests that they should each leave their clothes in a neat pile:

> 'If you leave your clothes tidy it will be so much easier to get dressed again, so put them the wight ray wound. Listen children! Did you hear me get my words mixed up? "The wight ray wound." Can you say that, what did I mean to say?'

Elsewhere, in another nursery classroom, the children are telling their teacher what they had for breakfast. The teacher is encouraging them to beat out the syllables in the phrases they say:

> 'Co/co/pops'
> 'Juice/and/toast'

In both cases, young children are being asked to disregard the message behind the words and to concentrate on the words themselves, so that they can reflect on the sound structure. In the first example, an opportunity has presented itself quite spontaneously but the second is a routine exercise to get children thinking about how words comprise 'chunks of sound'. That is, it is intended to trigger phonological awareness.

Phonological awareness refers to the set of skills which enables us to analyse the sounds in words we say and hear. A considerable amount of research evidence shows that early systematic introduction of activities designed to promote phonological awareness has a positive effect on later reading and spelling skills. But research conducted over many years, in different countries and across various languages has made remarkably little impact on classroom practice. Back in 1991, Benita Blachman reviewed the situation and commented sadly, 'despite the evidence, activities to build phonological awareness have not been routinely integrated into our kindergarten and first grade classrooms.' (Blachman, 1991: 53)

Although there is a clear commitment, when teaching young children, to enhancing their language experiences this does not regularly or explicitly include training in phonological awareness. There are many possible reasons for this apparent lack of transfer of strategies into the classroom teacher's repertoire. We believe that one explanation might be the relatively little attention paid, within research, to translating research findings into usable techniques which can be applied effectively in the 'real world' of the classroom.

The project from which this book has grown represented an attempt to implement a training and assessment programme for phonological awareness in ordinary classrooms. We took account of the practical needs of the teachers along with the demands and limitations of their work-place situations. Many of the teachers who were involved in our research project accepted that phonological awareness is important if children are to read and spell effectively. But, in common with many other teachers, they did not know enough about phonological awareness to build upon and to modify the activities which they were already using in their classrooms.

We found that by working collaboratively with us, teachers were able to take an active role in shaping features of the activities. The key to an active role is knowledge and in writing this book our aim is to enable our readers to gain a thorough working knowledge of phonological awareness. Readers should then in turn be well equipped:

- to understand that, however they are taught to read and spell, children must have an explicit awareness of the sounds in words;
- to acknowledge that it makes more sense to see that all children develop phonological awareness than to leave its development to chance;
- to grasp the principles which will form the basis of good practice;
- to put phonological awareness into context so that it becomes an integral part of teaching programmes, exploiting its role according to personal teaching strategies;
- to give phonological awareness a central place in improving the reading and spelling skills of children of all ages;
- to decide how best to promote the development of phonological awareness of poor readers and spellers.

Knowledge and resources: working together

We know from our experiences as practitioners that, while time pressures make it difficult to develop new work programmes and methods, teachers are continually adapting and modifying materials to tailor them to the needs of their pupils. The very fact that teachers put so much time and effort into these modifications illustrates how often published 'resource packs' and workbooks fall short of what is really required. We hope that having read this book and having gained sufficient knowledge about the nature and unique role of phonological awareness, readers will be able to elaborate and customise their own resources. Some ready-made, photocopiable resources are included to illustrate particular teaching points and strategies, but we fully expect readers to modify and interpret them in the light of knowledge acquired by working through this book.

We all recognise that there are many different aspects of reading and spelling to be considered when we are judging whether a child is competent in literacy. Before looking in more detail at phonological awareness we need to be clear about exactly which parts of the reading and spelling process are influenced by it.

It is sometimes assumed that learning to read and to spell is similar to learning to talk. The fact that not all spoken languages have a written form suggests that the situation is not as simple as that. Most children who grow up surrounded by spoken language go on to acquire it without focused or explicit instruction. This is not the case for written language. Left to their own devices, very few children will become proficient readers and spellers by themselves.

One fundamental skill for learning to read and to spell well is realising that spellings of words correspond with the spoken words which they represent. To do this the child must learn to analyse the words that they hear and the written-down words that they see.

In focusing on phonological awareness we are less concerned with the use of context or with reading comprehension although we would agree that they are important parts of the overall process. We are more concerned with how children can be helped to discover how our writing system works. The spelling of English is largely dependent on an alphabetic system where written letters represent the speech sounds of the spoken words. Teaching the skills which enable children to tackle this system should be a primary goal in the early years. For older pupils with written language difficulties it should be at the centre of remediation attempts. Through this book we hope that teachers (and other practitioners) will gain confidence in their knowledge and ability both to devise new teaching plans and to modify existing ones to achieve this goal.

Reading and spelling

Chapter 1

Segmenting Words:
The Rhyme and the Reason

This chapter provides a framework for the rest of the book by addressing a series of questions concerning the nature and origins of phonological awareness, and its links with spoken language. Phonological awareness has a firmly established role in written language use. We describe and illustrate this role, explaining key concepts and terms. In considering important concepts we identify issues relating to the teaching of reading which will be explored more fully in later chapters.

Young children become aware of the sounds in the words they hear and say as they acquire spoken language. At an early stage the child's knowledge about these sounds and the patterns and characteristics which link them is implicit. That is, understanding and producing the sounds that make up the stream of speech does not require conscious effort. We can draw a parallel with the way that a child may learn to hop or to climb without being consciously or explicitly aware of all the physical and perceptual processes involved in these activities.

What exactly is phonological awareness?

The earliest indications that children are reflecting on their own speech are heard in their word-play as in this example from a 3-year-old:

'Shirley Hughes? [children's author] . . . Curly Shoes!'

This child has juggled the sounds within the words even though her awareness of the structure of the phrases and of the words within them exists only at an implicit level.

As children mature and extend their familiarity with spoken language they become more aware of the similarities and differences between words and sounds. Their experiences with word games and nursery rhymes encourage them to reflect more deliberately on words so that they might be able, for example, to tell us that two words rhyme or 'sound the same'. These first demonstrations of explicit phonological awareness are usually evident well before children start to learn about 'written down' letters. Children delight in their early discovery of the similarities in sounds and this leads to a pleasurable repetition of the activity, so reinforcing the tendency to reflect on the intrinsic value of the speech sounds themselves, aside from their role in conveying sense and meaning.

Phonological awareness refers specifically to the child's realisation that the connected speech sounds that make up spoken language can be broken down into smaller segments, and that these segments can be manipulated. This sounds like a very formidable task for a child but, as we have seen, it is readily observed in the way that even pre-school children enjoy playing with whole words and speech-sounds. Adults notice word-play and smile, but they rarely recognise its significance.

Early word-play demonstrates phonological awareness

The sorts of variations that children introduce as they chant nursery rhymes are familiar to us all. For example:

> Hickory dickory dock
> The mouse ran up the sock

By manipulating rhymes in this way, rather than reciting learnt rhymes, children show that they understand that language can be segmented. They have begun to realise that continuous speech can be broken down into the segments we know as words. They can also break into the sound-structure of the words themselves:

> Eeny meeny miney moe
> Eeny teeny tiney toe
> Eeny weeny winey woe

Quite spontaneously this child has demonstrated a realisation that even smaller segments within words can be separated and manipulated; sounds can be deleted and others substituted.

All these games and the skills which underpin children's ability to carry them out arise from their experience of spoken language. Most young children can use these experiences, together with the knowledge gained from them, to reflect actively on the ways in which words can be divided.

Levels of phonological awareness

Mature users of spoken and written language demonstrate awareness of the sound structure of spoken language in a number of ways and at different levels. For example, many jokes, particularly puns, are the outcome of operating on the segments in words.

> *Teacher*: Give me a sentence, using the word, 'judicious'
> *Pupil*: Hands that /judicious/ [do dishes] can be soft as your face

But phonological awareness starts to emerge before children encounter print.

The diagram below summarises some of the ways of segmenting English words, and indicates how easy *or* difficult it is for a non-reader to gain access to these segments.

Segments of spoken words

SYLLABLES: *bis/cuit tel/e/phone pic/nic Thom/as*

syllables are very easily detected by most non-readers

ONSETS AND RIMES: *b/ike fr/idge spr/ing*

many non-readers are aware of the onset–rime division

PHONEMES: */c/.../a/.../p/; /s/.../o/.../k/; /b/.../r/.../u/.../sh/*

most non-readers cannot divide words into single phonemes

Syllables are the easiest segments in speech to detect. So, young children who have not yet encountered print can indicate the syllabic structure of words by nodding and beating out the rhythm of words. Interesting findings from studies of people who do not have a written language confirm that they also find syllable tasks relatively easy (Alegria and Morais, 1991).

Similarly, non-readers spontaneously segment syllables into onset (any consonant sounds which precede the vowel) and rime – the portion that includes the vowel sound and any consonants following it. Linguists have noted this tendency in native speakers making errors which are known as spoonerisms. The linguists assert that errors arise when speakers transpose *intact* onsets onto *intact* rimes, thus:

'Buy me some flandy coss!'

and not:

'Buy me some fandycloss/flondycass'.

They regard this as evidence that the junction between onset and rime has special significance for both speakers and listeners. The following examples show how words divide quite naturally into onset and rime.

Onsets and rimes

Onsets	*Rimes*
p	aw
p	ort
sp	ort
sh	ort
sh	ore
str	aw
	or
	ought

Remember, we are concerned here with the *sounds*
of syllables, not with their spellings.

We do not have to be literate to be aware that syllables divide in these ways because the syllabic divisions are created by peaks of acoustic energy which accompany vowel sounds in the speech stream. So syllabic and onset–rime divisions of the speech-stream are features of spoken language, and we register where these divisions are as part of the skill of understanding and producing speech, even though we are probably not directly aware that we have this knowledge. Unlike the syllable, however, individual phonemes cannot be acoustically isolated. That is, what appear to readers of alphabetic scripts as the smallest separate sounds in words cannot actually be separated without distortion. Try the following activity for yourself.

> Split the word 'house' into its separate phonemes. You should get three sounds which we will represent here by /h/.../ou/ .../s/.
>
> Now, put the three sounds back together again. You will find that you produce a poor approximation to the original word.

It seems that phoneme-by-phoneme segmentation, where individual speech sounds are marked out as separate items, is a difficult task and yet it is one that beginning reader/spellers might be asked to try before anyone knows whether or not they can perform the easier tasks that illustrate pre-reading phonological awareness.

Many researchers, including Lynette Bradley and Peter Bryant (Bryant and Bradley, 1985) and Usha Goswami (1995) have investigated the role of phonological awareness in a child's developing literacy skills, and they have focused on how children can be helped to link sound and spelling patterns. As we will describe in Chapter 3, Goswami, particularly, has shown how children can then use this knowledge to help them to make analogies between words or parts of words which are familiar and words which are new to them. Information about the findings of this research has enormous practical implications for the ways in which early reading and spelling skills are taught. We must not assume, however, that these researchers have discovered a 'new way for children to learn to read and spell'. Rather the research is discovering how children usually learn to read and to spell and is showing us more clearly the strategies which most children use. Our challenge, then, is to translate the knowledge about the process of learning to read and spell into strategies and programmes which will

> **Phonological awareness is not a passing trend**
>
> An awareness that spoken language can be broken into segments is obligatory if individuals are going to read and spell effectively. Research evidence only supports and explains what numerous teachers of pupils with literacy difficulties have been noticing for years.

make the whole process easier and more comprehensive for all children. Strategies based on our knowledge of what all effective, independent readers and spellers need to do will also equip us better for working with children who find the tasks more difficult than most.

It is fundamentally important, in the context of what this book sets out to achieve, to recognise that the terms 'phonological' and 'phonics' do *not* mean the same thing.

Phonology refers to a system of speech sounds. English, for example, uses only a small sample of the range of speech sounds which it is physically possible to produce. Native speakers of any language become implicitly aware of the sample of speech sounds which make up the system for their own language, and how they are combined and manipulated in meaningful speech. By the same token, 'foreign' or non-native words are immediately recognised as such, even without any further clues as to their origins.

For example: the Welsh phoneme which is represented, in spelling, with a double 'l' (as in *Llanelli*) is very difficult for non-Welsh speakers to make, but is instantly recognised by English speakers, for example, as being, 'non-English'. This skill is fundamental to understanding and producing spoken language.

Phonological awareness refers to the ability to focus, quite deliberately, on features of speech sounds. As we have already seen, this explicit awareness emerges gradually and becomes refined over time.

Phonics is a system for linking individual speech sounds – phonemes – with graphemes (letters or letter-patterns). The term is often applied to an instructional approach, in which the link is explained to novice readers–spellers. More recently, many 'phonics' approaches have taken account of the difficulties which young children can experience in trying to link single letters with single sounds. 'New Phonics' will be considered in later chapters, but for the moment we want to emphasise that both traditional and new phonic approaches require the learner to be primed by being sensitive to the phonological structure of spoken words.

Over the years many different methods have been adopted for teaching literacy skills. Alongside these we know, from investigations into the processes involved in reading and writing, that there is a steady accumulation of strategies which seem to account for effective skills in mature readers. The strategies may be attributed partly to a reader's experience (including classroom teaching) but partly to the individual's unfolding problem-solving skills. One researcher who has described the developmental progression is Uta Frith (Frith, 1985). According to her view, most children start to read by recalling word shapes which they have stored in their visual memory. That is, they respond to the overall appearance of the word or to what they perceive as its salient features. This approach often produces some

What is the difference between phonological awareness and phonics?

Does phonological awareness have a role however reading and spelling are taught, or is it only important for phonics?

surprising results. For example, researchers working with Linnea Ehri (Ehri, 1987) reported that young children who could read environmental print failed to notice the difference between 'XEPSI' and 'PEPSI' when the words were presented in their familiar, commercial format. These children were using an approach to reading which has come to be termed 'logographic' because written words are treated like Chinese characters, undifferentiated patterns or logographs. In the classroom we support the 'Look-and-Say' strategy:

- with flash-cards
- by placing labels on furniture and objects
- by training visual skills in preparation for reading.

As a gentle introduction and for teaching children to recognise a limited set of frequently encountered written words with irregular spelling-patterns, a 'Look-and-Say' approach is effective.

Otherwise, a logographic strategy is very soon shown to be inadequate for independent reading because the apprentice reader needs the support of a fluent reader to help with all the unknown words. Sometimes the context can provide the clues but again, as the child's reading experience widens the range of possibilities for any new word is extended, and guessing is progressively less successful, as the following example shows:

'When I am rich I will buy a house' ('When I am rich I will buy a horse')

Eventually, the strain on the child's visual memory becomes insupportable and new strategies are needed to supplement a recognition of word shapes. When children have been in school for a while they may start to notice similarities in letter combinations which correspond to similarities in speech sounds, and, as Goswami suggests, use an analogy strategy to decode unfamiliar words.

'When I am rich I will buy a ... [it looks like 'mouse'...] ...house!'

But, as Uta Frith points out, once children start to encode or spell an alphabetic approach is unavoidable. The recognition of a known word from its written-down equivalent might be achieved on the basis of partial decoding, together with context-inspired guessing:

'.../p/.../a/.../r/.../a/... parachute!'

However, to retrieve the written equivalent of a spoken word – a spelling – the apprentice writer must do one of the following:

- copy a model
- rote-learn a sequence of letter-names: '...O...N...C...E... "once"'
- break down the word into a sequence of phonemes and attach the letters which are known to represent each phoneme.

Neither of the first two strategies allows young writers the independence to attempt words they have previously only heard. While the third may not result in conventional spellings it can generate good readable alternatives which *could* represent spoken words.

In Frith's view, in attending to the alphabetic nature of *spelling* the child is prompted to apply the same set of principles to *reading*. In this way, an alphabetic strategy for reading supplements – but does not replace – the earlier logographic strategy.

Once apprentice readers–spellers have cracked the alphabetic code they are free to decode and encode written language for themselves. Given greater access to the written and printed word wherever they encounter it – on cereal packets, on signs in buildings, through TV commercials, as well as in the classroom – they can continue to practise their new-found skills until they can be applied automatically. With increased exposure and more practice they will develop sophisticated skills, particularly what Frith calls an orthographic strategy. This involves applying the complex rules which are part of the English spelling system. For example, we know 'automatically' that no English word ends with a 'J', and we will read the letter C as /s/ when it is followed by certain vowel-letters. We are more likely to build up such knowledge of the spelling system through the experience of reading and writing than by direct instruction. After all, we have very few rules like this:

'I' before 'E'
Except after 'C'

Apprentices find the key to written language competence when they make the links between sounds that they hear and letters that they see. Clearly the process of discovery can be helped by the instructional approach adopted in the classroom. That is, teaching can make the letter–sound link for the child who has already discovered that spoken language can be divided into chunks. Without appropriate teaching, children must make the link for themselves just as, with experience, they are expected to unravel the intricacies of the spelling-system. Later, we will see that, for some children, with or without teaching that demonstrates how the alphabet works, the alphabetic principle remains a mystery.

We advocate that, in order to reduce the incidence of literacy failure, teaching approaches for all young children should address the skills which support phonologically based strategies before reading and spelling problems can emerge.

However, where literacy difficulties have become entrenched older pupils will probably show evidence of having failed to break through the alphabetic barrier. Consequently they will not have access to the range of strategies which allow rapid, accurate and versatile reading and writing. Closer examination of their difficulties often reveal:

- poor rhyming skills
- laborious letter-by-letter word attack skills
- restricted use of analogies with known words
- difficulties in recalling the correct sequences of letters
- haphazard or bizarre combinations of letters to represent sound structures.

Where older pupils are struggling with reading and spelling it will be essential to consider the underlying competencies which may be lacking in these individuals, and to take account of phonological weaknesses in a remediation programme.

> **Where does phonological awareness fit in current approaches to teaching reading and spelling?**
>
> Phonological awareness is necessary for readers to make full use of the alphabetic principle which underpins our written language system. However reading and spelling are taught, we all need to understand that letters and letter-patterns represent units of sound, and, prior to this, that spoken words are made up of units of sound.

Is phonological awareness really so crucial?

Phonological awareness alone is obviously not the only skill which children need to become fully literate. We acknowledge that there is a wide range of skills, strategies and prior knowledge that readers bring to the task of processing written language. But they cannot proceed unless they can read and write single words. According to the orthography or spelling-system of English, as well as that of many other European languages, single words are broken into their component sounds and then the letters of the alphabet are used as a code to represent those sounds. Contrary to what some pundits would have us believe, this most definitely continues to have a place in maintaining and extending the reading and spelling capabilities of all written language-users so we want to take this opportunity to dispel certain myths suggesting alternative views about skilled reading:
- Skilled readers do not look at every letter when reading: **Wrong!**
- Skilled readers make greater use of context to read words: **Wrong!**
- Skilled readers do not use phonological strategies to read: **Wrong!**

Skilled readers *do* look at every letter

Intuition and examination of our own approaches to reading could persuade us that, as effective readers and writers, we simply remember a word-shape for every word which we need to read, much as the XEPSI/PEPSI logographic readers do. While we do carry in our heads, lexicons or personal dictionaries which contain thousands of entries, each entry is closely specified. Consider the following:

compete/complete
extant/extent
noisily/nosily
thorough/through
even/ever

If you were operating on the basis of visual shapes and patterns, without any regard to the component letters, misreadings and confusion would be highly likely. But, it might be argued, the specification of a sequence of letters as one particular word is normally decided by its place in the context of continuous text. It seems, in fact, that context plays a small part only in determining the decoding of individual words.

Skilled readers actually make *less* use, than poor readers, of context for reading words

Skilled readers identify words on the basis of letter patterns which they link with sound patterns. These, in turn, combine to produce spoken words which then reveal meaning. Skilled readers use context to *interpret* words and they are able to process text much more quickly because they rapidly comprehend its message, as in the following example:

> The old man was content to live alone with his memories.
> The content of the letter did not interest her.

Conversely, poorer readers are using their 'processing space' to work out what individual letter configurations represent, by the application of a more limited range of strategies, for example, a visual approach alone.

Skilled readers *do* use phonological strategies for spelling

Skilled written language users seem to spell almost automatically. However, when words become complex, or they are unusual or unfamiliar it will be necessary for every speller to fall back on syllabification (breaking a spoken word into component syllables). Try spelling *deoxyribonucleic* (acid) or *antidisestablishment* without splitting the words into syllables!

Despite large reading vocabularies or lexicons, we still encounter new words, for example, the brand-names of new commodities, unusual place-names or family-names. In particular, when we embark on new subject areas in secondary or tertiary education or in professional training there is a new vocabulary to be learned.

Acquiring written language competence has been modelled on the ascent of a ladder but our view is that it also involves collecting a bag of tools during the ascent. Progress is marked by the gradual accumulation of skills and strategies for decoding and encoding written language. The application of the different competencies becomes automatic but selective, so that we know when to deploy visual skills alone or phonological skills alone, or in conjunction. Once we have kicked away the ladder, the tools are still there to serve us in all our reading and spelling needs.

> **How can we be sure that phonological awareness is so crucial?**
>
> Although phonological awareness is not *sufficient* to guarantee the acquisition and consolidation of secure reading and writing skills, it is *necessary*. Without a sensitivity to the sound structure of language we cannot progress to using the alphabetic approach which underpins our spelling-system.

Summary

This chapter provides a framework for the rest of the book by:
- introducing key terms
- identifying a role for phonological awareness at the interface between spoken and written language
- examining concepts and issues which are known to give rise to some confusion and may be surrounded by myth
- setting out what is firmly established about the acquisition of strategies for reading and writing.

In the next chapter we will begin the process of putting phonological awareness back into context. That is, starting with the pre-school years, we will address the possibility of promoting phonological awareness through a fresh look at the pre-reading curriculum.

Chapter 2

Rhyme Awareness: A Pre-reading Skill

In the previous chapter we stressed how important it is for apprentice written language-users to be aware that spoken language can be segmented. We also explained that this phonological awareness starts to emerge alongside spoken language development. In the present chapter we focus on the phonological skills and activities that are within the ability range of most young pre-readers. We propose ways in which teachers and nursery nurses can enhance the development of phonological awareness and suggest that parents too can nurture these skills.

There is an impressive body of research evidence which confirms that children's knowledge of nursery rhymes when they are three-and-a-half years old is a good predictor of their ability to make judgements on the onsets and rimes of words before they go to school. If they recognise when words start with the same sound or when they rhyme, without knowing anything about the alphabet they will be well prepared for the task ahead. Morag Maclean, working with Peter Bryant and Lynette Bradley (Maclean, Bryant and Bradley, 1987) established that this relationship between early nursery rhyme knowledge and pre-school phonological awareness held true regardless of the intelligence levels and social background of the children.

Just because researchers are able to demonstrate a statistical relationship between knowing nursery rhymes and having good phonological awareness we should not assume that nursery rhyme knowledge *produces* good phonological awareness. After all, children who find it easy to learn nursery rhymes might have all-round efficient phonological processing abilities. What we can be sure of is:

Nursery rhymes

> Nursery rhymes, as well as other jingles and word-games, act as a *trigger* for raising phonological awareness to an explicit level.

So let us consider what is so special about how adults and children share nursery rhymes:

- The adult makes it clear that the language itself is the game, and that the words and sounds of the rhymes or jingles can be explored and enjoyed for their own sake, outside the context of conveying information.

- Enjoying rhymes with an adult is one of the few remaining opportunities for little children to engage in an exclusively listening activity. An increasing number of pre-school activities, even those which are directed at listening skills, often involve a visual component either as a support, reinforcement or reward. This is undoubtedly an asset in some situations but opportunities should also be created purely for listening if children are to develop a working knowledge of the way in which speech is made up of segments of sound.

- When reciting nursery rhymes with children most adults emphasise the rhythm, usually accentuating this with body movement, gesture and tone of voice. These physical reinforcers focus the child's interest and attention on the qualities of the words and sounds in the rhyme or jingle.

- The strong rhythm of nursery rhymes acts as a signal to the child that something interesting is about to happen in the sounds of the words. The 'something interesting' is, of course, the rhyming word. In other words, the stress pattern leads the listener to an expectation of rhyme.

- Rhymes, jingles and other word play can accompany a wide range of activities which children and adults share. No special equipment is needed and there seems to be 'a rhyme for everything' where almost all children's routines and daily events can be enhanced by a rhyme or by word play. Traditional nursery rhymes are often linked with particular events 'One, Two/Buckle my shoe' is often linked with dressing. Personalised rhymes are also spontaneously generated, for example, 'splish, splash, splosh, have a nice wash' might accompany bath time.

In sharing rhyming games and routines with an adult, a child will begin to reflect actively on the structural qualities which make them such fun. With further practice, they discover the qualities which set these games apart from the type of language which is used to form questions, make demands, share knowledge and so on.

> Language play, especially that which is shared with an adult, raises a latent ability to a level of active exploration and reflection.

Different levels of phonological awareness were described in Chapter 1. It was also suggested that phoneme awareness – that is, an ability to recognise and manipulate the smallest segments of syllables – is usually beyond the capabilities of non-readers. In recognition that phonemes are the segments which are more or less represented by alphabetic letters, many studies have included phoneme awareness in pre-school phonological training routines. A necessary component of such studies has been the inclusion of letters and some instruction in letter–sound correspondence.

However, we recognise that many pre-school groups deliberately de-emphasise alphabetic letters because their pupils may go on to different schools with varying approaches to the teaching of literacy. Moreover, in our view, a compelling reason for not attempting to address phoneme awareness is that this level of analysis draws on cognitive competencies which are largely beyond many 4 year olds. Accordingly, they cannot be trained, even with plastic letters, to 'perform' at this level without extensive, focused input which requires specialist training of teachers.

Furthermore, following studies into pre-school training programmes, many practitioners have felt they should address, not only rime awareness, but onset awareness, as part of a phonological awareness programme. In our own study, that from which this book has grown, we featured training routines which targeted rime awareness only. This was because, although young children *can* recognise onsets, for them, rimes are far more accessible: the rime is usually a larger unit of sound, it begins with and contains the vowel which is, relative to consonants, less influenced by surrounding sounds and therefore more stable. (The acoustic features of language segments are considered in more detail in Chapter 4.) Additionally, training children to attend to rimes does not 'clash' with anything in their past experience which may have included, for example, alphabet friezes that feature, not onsets, but the initial letter sounds associated with written-down words. The recommendations relating to early phonological training in this book follow the same guiding principle: the level of segmentation which young children find the easiest should be the starting-point for encouraging children to make judgements about the sounds in words.

> We believe that children's phonological awareness can be raised to a level that supports early reading and spelling acquisition without reference to alphabetic letters.

Nursery-class routines and phonological awareness

Introducing a phonological awareness training programme: points to consider

Given the pressure of time and the limited resources available to teachers it is essential that, if changes are to be made or initiatives taken, classroom innovation must have relevance for all children and must make a real difference.

It is therefore important to consider both the demands which new initiatives might make and the capabilities of the children for whom they are intended. In connection with the latter we have already emphasised that certain phonological tasks may be far too difficult for the majority of 4 year olds because they call on skills which very young children simply do not possess. Instead, there are many tasks which address prerequisite skills, and have long-term and significant benefits.

To illustrate this, let us consider an analogy with gross motor development: most children learn to crawl before progressing to walking. Crawling is valuable in itself for establishing important motor patterns and for giving the child the opportunity to grow in confidence before gradually adopting an upright posture.

Similarly establishing awareness of the onset–rime division before the child formally encounters letters and letter-patterns, provides a firm foundation for, not merely a bridge to, later reading and spelling.

A major practical issue in the nursery class is the wide variation in the age ranges of the children; in their developmental levels, and their experiences. A well-designed programme can provide a framework for locating individual children in terms of their developmental progression, and for identifying those who may need more focused help.

> A pre-reading programme should include a component for establishing the phonological skills which most young children could reasonably be expected to develop with minimal support and which teachers, without special training, can address. All the evidence suggests that pre-readers need a grounding in activities that promote rhyme awareness, thus preparing them for cracking the alphabetic code.

Do children need more than nursery rhymes?

Could it be that all that is needed is for children to participate in the nursery-rhyme activities that are part-and-parcel of the nursery-class routine?

Most pre-school classes have group language activities, usually conducted 'on the mat'. Children sit on the floor and an adult leads them in chanting rhymes and acting out action rhymes, to offer just two examples. The children's enjoyment of this part of the nursery routine is obvious, and it provides opportunities for social participation. But the structure of this activity, in which the emphasis is on *group* participation, means that as long as children appear to be part of the group there is no reason to check on the details of what they are learning, nor is there any mechanism for conducting this check.

> If the focus of the activity is learning to recite the jingle or
> nursery rhyme we have to be sure that every child has learned it.

In the study referred to earlier, Morag Maclean and her colleagues (Maclean, Bryant and Bradley, 1987) established that the following traditional rhymes are known to most English-speaking pre-schoolers:

Humpty-Dumpty sat on the wall
Baa-Baa Black Sheep
Twinkle Twinkle Little Star
Hickory Dickory Dock
Jack and Jill went up the hill

Therefore, where these rhymes have regularly been included in 'Talk-time', teachers could reasonably expect every child to be able to recite them. Occasionally, a child can be observed making some token contribution to the group recitation but, when asked, will relate the story of the rhyme without any acknowledgement that what they have heard every day was in rhyming verse. The teacher should be concerned about this child's phonological awareness.

'Talk-time' is only one part of the nursery routine where rhymes and other language-based games might appear. Language activities can be tackled in many contexts, using different media. In the next section we will consider some ways of incorporating phonological training within the pre-school curriculum, outside the context of literacy instruction. In describing each activity we will emphasise certain key aspects to be observed, both in connection with the examples given here and with activities based on them.

Promoting phonological awareness in young pre-readers

It has already been suggested that before young children can begin to make judgements on the sound structure of language they have to realise, quite explicitly, that language can be an object of study in itself. If you ask many of these children about the beginning sound of 'cat' they will answer, 'miaow'. That is, they cannot focus on the form of language, only on the messages which it conveys. **But before they can begin to tackle this they must be able to listen!** The game, *If-I-say-your-name* (see Activity 1, page 19), focuses specifically on children's listening skills. This type of activity provides clear opportunities to check whether individual children are effective listeners. Children who consistently fail to listen properly, for any reason, will need special support to complete tasks where listening is an essential component. We will return to this issue in the next chapter when we consider children who have difficulties with any listening routines.

In Chapter 1 we mentioned that segmenting words, syllable-by-syllable, is one of the earliest indications that children are attending to their sound-structure. In many classes children are already given some opportunity to show that they can split words up in this way. They often accompany this type of activity by head-nodding, stamping their feet, banging their fists. In *What did you eat today?* (Activity 2, page 20), we offer some suggestions for enhancing these skills where they have already begun to emerge in groups of children, but suggest targeting individual children to identify those who are having difficulty at this level.

A key issue when introducing children to any routines in which language itself is the object of study is their understanding of the concept, and use of the label, 'word'. A word is an abstract notion and so is very difficult for a child who is functioning at a concrete level. *Rhyming riddles* (Activity 3, page 21) performs a dual function in introducing children to words and to rhymes.

Once the concept of rhyming words has been established there are many rhyming games for children to play. First, however, it is important to distinguish between different types of rhyming activities so that the teacher is aware of exactly what demands are being made of the children. In general, rhyming activities divide into three categories:

1. *Rhyme judgement* – The easiest rhyming game, the child is asked, 'Do these words rhyme?' and the response is either 'Yes' or 'No'. Obviously there is plenty of scope for guessing at this level.
2. *Rhyme detection* – In these games the child has to select, from given alternatives, a word which rhymes (or does not rhyme) when compared with other words.
3. *Rhyme production or generation* – A very difficult task, particularly for a non-reader, the most demanding version requires children to supply rhymes to a given stimulus word.

The activities which we are including here focus, firstly, on rhyme detection. As with all rhyming activities it is important that the children are reminded about what rhymes are and that they verbalise (say) the words to which they are attending. It is not enough that they hear the teacher say the words or that they look at pictures illustrating the words. Remember to refer only to *words* rhyming, not pictures or objects.

In Activity 4, *Favourite Foods* (page 22), children must decide which word from a selection rhymes with the target, and in Activity 5, *Odd-one-out* (page 24), they have to choose a group of words which *do* rhyme, and then isolate one which *does not*.

Activity 6 (page 26) is designed to encourage children to produce rhyming words for themselves. There is a limit to the number of rhymes there are for every word as long as you are using real words. So, *The Picnic Game* uses made-up words. A clear pattern is established which gives the child lots of clues about the rhyming word. In suggested variations on that game there are fewer clues and many children will find these much more difficult. Don't forget, when older children and adults are asked to produce lists of rhyming words (either real or nonsense) they will usually split off the rime and, working through the alphabet, add consonant sounds to generate new words. Pre-reading children do not have this framework to support them.

Most parents are concerned that their children should learn to read and spell. While recognising that formal instruction in reading and spelling is the teacher's domain parents can be encouraged to help their children to develop the foundation skills for written language, and so make a valuable contribution to the process. There are many good reasons to offer parents which explain why they have a special role in helping their children to develop good phonological awareness:

- Phonological awareness is firmly rooted within the spoken language skills which first emerge in child–parent exchanges.
- Phonological awareness usually develops well before, and independently of, the formal teaching of reading and spelling.
- If phonological awareness is well established reading and spelling are comparatively easy to teach. Without this skill there is a limit on how far a child can progress in written language.
- Early promotion of phonological awareness does not encroach upon or clash with reading and spelling schemes.
- Word play can be personalised in the home and can become special for the child, particularly if rhyming games include family, pet or friends' names.
- Parents of the younger or less able children in the Reception class can make a significant difference by promoting the pre-literacy skills of those children not yet ready for formal reading and spelling tasks.

The following page can be photocopied and given to parents to encourage them to take an active role in developing these important skills.

Parents and phonological awareness

All rhymes help children to notice patterns in words.
They use these patterns to help them to read and to spell.

EVERY DAY   RHYME PLAY

Great big feet and knobbly knees
I've got sausages, chips and ____.

Splish, splash, splosh
Have a nice wash

Our rhyme ... for bathtime!

Let's put on something
that sounds like *clock*.

Some other ideas:

1. Listen to and say all sorts of nursery rhymes, number rhymes and action rhymes.

2. Play rhyming games like 'I hear with my little ear, something that rhymes with ...'

3. Make up stories of rhyming words including nonsense words.

Activity 1: If-I-say-your-name

Instructions

This is a variation on the 'Simon-Says' game for children in a group. Explain that the children must carry out an action *only* when their name is called out. Be careful not to give any extra cues to the child, for example, by looking directly at the named child.

    Example: 'Put your finger on your chin … William.'

Key elements

- Naming the child *after the instruction is given* encourages them to listen to the whole command.
- Removing additional cues such as eye-pointing and gesture focuses attention on listening skills.

Remember, persistent failure might indicate:

- poor hearing
- general inattentiveness
- poor levels of attention for group activities
- difficulty in responding to verbal information which is unsupported by visual cues
- difficulty with remembering instructions.

Activity 2: What did you eat today?

This activity is presented within the group but it is important that each child is asked to make an individual response.

Instructions
The teacher models a response, by saying 'For breakfast I had ... tea/and/toast' and emphasising the beats, marks them by clapping, tapping.

Then, each child is asked in turn, 'What did you have for breakfast/lunch?'

Key elements
- Whatever means are used for the child to indicate syllables should not distract the child from the task. For example, children can get carried away by clapping and even more so by using musical instruments. Tapping lightly on a table may be more successful.
- It is a good idea to reinforce a correct response by asking the rest of the group to copy.
- Where this is a new task for children it is important to give them plenty of practice.

Variations
This activity lends itself to practice and reinforcement in a wide variety of settings. For example, when discussing an item that a child has brought in to 'show', children's attention can be drawn to the name of the item, by beating out the syllables: con/ker; yel/low/flow/er. In 'Newstime' a child often tells the name of a new brother or sister, or a new pet: Ol/iv/er; Rob/in/son. The whole group can then practise the new name.

Activity 3: Rhyming riddles

This group activity has two levels. It is important to start with the easier level and to establish that all children can achieve a correct response before moving on to the higher level (see variations).

Instructions
Teacher says: 'I am thinking of a word. It means a furry animal that catches mice and it rhymes with "mat".'

Key elements
- At this level the definition must be completely unambiguous so that children could guess the word from the definition.
- A variation on the target word, for example, 'puss' is not allowable, nor even 'nearly right'. If it does not rhyme it is incorrect.
- If a rhyming word which does not fit the definition is offered the child should be praised for finding a rhyming word but the inaccuracy should be explained.

Variations
I hear with my little ear: 'a *word* that rhymes with *more*' (*floor*). In this version the teacher targets an object in the classroom.

Rhyming box: The teacher collects objects in a box and gives a clue based on rhyme. When children guess correctly the object is shown to the group. Give credit for good rhyming alternatives even if it is unlikely that a named object could be in the box.

Activity 4: Favourite foods

For this you will need two sets of illustrations, one set featuring various creatures, the other, food or drink. You can take coloured pictures from the classroom. Alternatively, you can photocopy and enlarge those provided, stick them to card and cut them into single pictures.

Instructions

> 'All of these animals have favourite things to eat and drink. But their real favourites sound like/rhyme with their names. Let's say the names of all their favourite things ..."pear, carrot, pie ..."'
> (until all the food/drink pictures have been named)

The teacher then places, in front of the children, four pictures from the food selection.

> 'Let's say the words that go with these things – pear, carrot, rice, roll'

The teacher holds up a picture from the animal selection:

> 'This is Polly Parrot – listen, Polly Parrot. Her favourite food rhymes with / sounds like her name. Polly Parrot likes a ...?'

(Choose a child who is likely to be able to demonstrate this correctly.)

> 'Carrot! Well done, Daniel. Listen, everybody ...'Polly Parrot likes a carrot' ... it rhymes. Now someone else ..."

Ask the children to chant the four 'food' words each time:

Sammy Snake likes some ...	(cake, rice, carrot, roll)
Larry Lamb likes some ...	(cake, roll, rice, jam)
Monty Mole likes some ...	(pie, jam, roll, carrot)
Millions of mice like lots of ...	(jam, rice, roll, cake)
Bobby Bear likes a ...	(carrot, cheese, pear, pie)

Key elements
- You should not write on the pictures or draw attention to the written versions of the names, in any way.
- The selection of food words should be randomised so that children do not try to solve the puzzle according to the position of the pictures.
- You can create as many animals as you like, and find rhyming foods. You are not constrained by words that have the same spelling patterns as the target word (name of the animal).

Activity 5: Odd-one-out

You will need illustrations for this activity, either pictures which you have collected or you can copy those provided.

Instructions
Give alternate children a piece of A4 paper on which is drawn a circle or a triangle. Then give the children with the circles, four pictures, representing the words *bee*, *key*, *knee* and *pear*. Give the children with triangles, four different pictures for the words *fox*, *box*, *socks* and *kite*. Rehearse the words that go with the pictures, making sure that the non-rhyming distracter is in a different place in the two lists. Then say to the children with circles, 'Say your words. Put the pictures that go with the rhyming words *inside* the circle. Put the odd-one-out *outside* the circle.' Do the same with the other group, substituting the word 'triangle' for 'circle'.

Each child can stick down the pictures once they are known to be correctly placed. They can also be coloured. Afterwards, ask individual children why 'that one' is outside the circle/triangle.

Key elements
* Try to stop the children copying from one another, by alternating circles and triangles and giving them different selections of pictures.
* If you use your own words note the structure of the specimen words. That is, all the words are one-syllable; they start with a single consonant *sound*. Open syllables (those ending in a vowel *sound*) and closed syllables (those ending in a consonant *sound*) are not mixed.

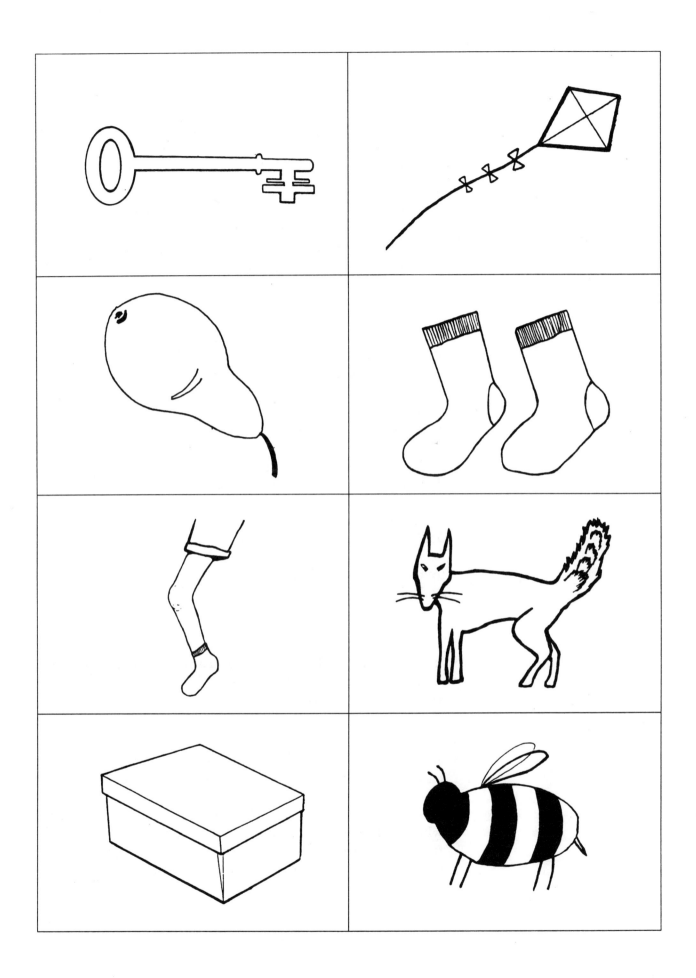

Activity 6: The Picnic Game

Instructions

You may like to set up the game using a favourite character, puppet or doll. If this is the case it would be useful to focus on the name of the character to establish the idea of rhyme by first producing lots of words and nonsense words which rhyme with the name.

> 'We're going to play a game with words. We're going to pretend that we're going on a picnic (with character if using) and we've got lots of things to remember. But I've lost the words that go with the things we need to take! See if you can help me find the words.
>
> Dutter, mutter, gutter, rutter
> Shall we take some bread and … (butter)?
>
> Welly, belly, melly, telly
> Here's a nice big wobbly … (jelly)
>
> Lickin, pickin, tickin, kickin
> We need lots of cold roast … (chicken)
>
> Riskits, tiskits, miskits, wiskits
> Shall we have some chocolate … (biscuits)?
>
> Pogurt, nogurt, sogurt, wogurt
> Don't forget the pots of … yoghurt
>
> Toffee, noffee, boffee, doffee
> And now for Mum, a cup of … coffee'

Key elements

- It is important to set up a pattern and an expectation of rhyme.
- This works well as a group activity but each child should be given the opportunity to respond.

Variations

- The choice of words can easily be arranged according to preference. Rhyming nonsense words add to the fun and give semantic freedom.
- The game can be extended. For example, children could make whispered suggestions to the teacher about what they would like to take. The teacher then helps them to generate rhyming words so that the rest of the group can guess what the secret item is.

- The game can be adapted easily to reflect events that have current significance for the class:
  - a school outing
  - a Spring Fair
  - going swimming
  - going on holiday.

Rhyming table

Topic, or other interest, tables are a common feature of many early years classrooms. This kind of presentation lends itself to extending the rhyming theme. One suggestion might be to present a few items, some with rhyming partners *...phone/stone...box/socks* and others without. The children are invited to suggest, select or bring from home, items with rhyming names. Alternatively, some children could draw pictures of items with rhyming names.

In this chapter we have outlined a broad range of suggestions for games which, as we know from experience, can easily be accommodated within the nursery routine and which are enjoyed by most children around the age of 4 or 5. It is important, in all these games, to make sure that every child is fully participating and not to assume that because an activity was regularly carried out in class, all participating children will be competent in the relevant skill area.

In the next chapter we consider those children who may not be gaining full benefit from such activities, and what additional support these children might need.

Chapter 3

Poor Rhyming Skills in Young Children

Chapter 2 considered ways in which parents, teachers and other professionals can promote the development of phonological awareness in young children before they begin to read and spell. The abilities described there and the activities designed to promote them are within the capacity of most non-reading young children.

The ability to detect rhyme indicates an awareness of the onset–rime division. Children who remain insensitive to this division, despite ample opportunity to practise rhyming skills, may be at risk of experiencing difficulties with reading and spelling. Some of these children, even when they have taken part in activities targeting phonological awareness, do not acquire rhyming and other phonological skills as well as might be expected. For them the difficulty seems to be out of step with their usual facility for learning.

The current chapter focuses on these children, how to identify them and how to help them.

The importance of developing early phonological awareness is being increasingly recognised by producers of commercial resources, and many schools now include activities in their pre-reading and early reading curriculum for promoting children's awareness of rhymes. But maximising the benefits of early phonological training involves creating opportunities for *all children* to become skilled in making judgements about the sounds in words, and it involves creating opportunities for teachers to discover which children might need further help. So it is important to stress that where *group* activities are the norm in pre-school and early reception settings, every child must

Identifying poor phonological skills

> It is very easy for children, particularly those who are bright and chatty, to 'slip through the net'. Rhyming skills, and other markers of phonological awareness, are not easily detected unless you listen carefully to how every child responds to language games.

have the opportunity to make an individual response, when it comes to phonological routines. Simply chanting nursery rhymes or marking syllables or having a 'rhyming table display' in the classroom is not enough in itself.

We can discover which children are not developing the phonological skills which form the foundations for effective reading and spelling by asking them, **individually**, to demonstrate these skills. At this early stage we still have the time and the opportunity to provide extra help for those children who need it, before formal instruction in reading and spelling begins, and, most importantly, before an early weakness can be translated into literacy failure.

A feature of this chapter will be the presentation of 'mini case studies' describing a number of children with different patterns of phonological abilities and overall learning ability. We will also suggest ways in which typical profiles might best be identified and individual needs met. But first, let's consider briefly some of the factors, relating both to general development and to more specific difficulties, which may underpin poor phonological awareness.

Why children might fail to demonstrate phonological awareness

Most children will respond to classroom routines to promote their awareness of the sound segments in words, but we must accept that, as with every skill, children vary in the amount of practice needed before skills are fully established. Similarly, while there are 'all-rounders' – children who grasp every new concept and area of learning, apparently without effort – most children struggle at some time, and with some task. This is where a teacher's experience, both of children in general and of individual children in a class, is invaluable in discriminating between those who need focused help and those who simply need more practice. Possible reasons for children's inability to respond appropriately to rhyming games, for example, are considered below to assist that decision-making process.

General maturity

An obvious factor affecting children's ability to respond to activities such as those described in Chapter 2 is their general level of cognitive or intellectual maturity. Where children appear to be generally delayed, that is, they experience more difficulty with all games and tasks than the majority of children in the class, we would expect them to take longer to respond appropriately to phonological routines. At the same time, these children will probably exhibit behaviour – social, emotional, motoric and linguistic – which is more appropriate to a younger child. In the context of the case studies below we refer to these children as developmentally delayed.

Listening and attention

The activities or games which we described in Chapter 2 clearly depend to some considerable extent on children's ability to listen closely or attend to what is being said. In fact **Activity 1** (page 19) is primarily concerned with establishing good listening behaviour, and we listed there some factors which could explain a child's failure in this task: general inattentiveness, poor attention to group-based activities, a general reluctance to attend when activities don't feature pictures or other visual cues, or poor hearing. With regard to the latter point it is important to realise that intermittent hearing loss is quite common in young children and occasionally may require medical attention, but poor listening skills and poor hearing acuity are not necessarily always linked. Therefore, it is worth practising *If-I-Say-Your-Name* to try and address the other likely causes of poor attention. Teachers, many of whom deplore what they regard as a general deterioration in children's ability to listen, frequently have their own 'ploys' for gaining pupil's attention in preparation for some focused listening task, such as registration. In one nursery classroom, for example, the teacher introduces a special puppet whenever she needs the children to attend solely to what she's saying. The puppet is on show for the duration of the time in which the children must listen for instructions, and its head starts to retract into its body if any child visibly starts to drift 'off task', when the teacher comments, 'Somebody's not listening!'.

At the same time we must also consider the possibility that some children find phonological tasks difficult because they have a wider language problem. Sometimes this may be quite evident and severe enough to warrant referral to speech and language therapy services. For other children it may simply appear, to teachers and parents, as a mild delay, or may even go unnoticed, only gaining significance in the light of concern about the child's struggle to develop phonological awareness. In other cases, children may have already received attention to their problems by attending for therapy but have been discharged because their spoken language skills have developed to an age-appropriate level.

Spoken language difficulties

In the previous paragraph we raised the possibility that difficulties with promoting phonological awareness *may* occur in connection with spoken language difficulties. The range of spoken language problems is wide and the underlying reasons for them are many and varied: some children arrive in school communicating in a telegraphic fashion, unable to talk in connected sentences. Others can be understood but have a significant language delay, sounding like a very much younger child and understanding only very simple instructions. In other cases there may be physical or structural limitations on the way the child produces speech sounds, as in, for example, cleft palate or specific muscular weakness.

However, others will be difficult to understand because they have not yet developed and organised a coherent speech sound system. Not all spoken language problems will be associated with poor phonological awareness but for this latter group there *is* likely to be an association and the two are linked via weaknesses – delays or disorders – in the phonological processing domain. The phonological processing system has a key role in enabling the speaker to interpret the rules governing the organisation of speech sounds in a given language. For developing phonological awareness the speaker must bring this processing role to an explicit level reflecting actively on patterns of speech sounds. If the underlying phonological processing system is not functioning effectively enough to support the development of an adequate speech sound system it certainly cannot provide the foundation for phonological judgements.

In considering phonological skills in this way, a picture emerges where speech and language therapists and teachers might be separately addressing two aspects of the same underlying difficulties.

> 'The speech therapist clearly has a critical role ... of identifying the at-risk child and promoting pre-reading and spelling skills since the dyslexics of the future are in speech therapy clinics now.' (Stackhouse, 1989)

We would add to this that teachers working with children with poor phonological awareness would be well advised to probe spoken language development, and to liaise with a speech and language therapist wherever this is possible.

While local organisation of both education and health services make it inappropriate for us to be prescriptive we would advocate that teachers and speech and language therapists explore, within their own practice, the possibilities for working collaboratively. In this partnership they can consider together the dual role of the phonological processing system – its significance for spoken language, and, through phonological awareness, for the development of written language skills. Furthermore, they can work together to support children with phonological processing difficulties and jointly promote both spoken and written language.

Teachers and therapists need to work collaboratively to support some children

- Spoken language development and some of the skills underpinning written language are closely associated.
- Children with resolved spoken language difficulties may continue to have difficulties making phonological judgements.
- Aspects of therapeutic techniques from the clinic and teaching approaches from the classroom can be adapted and applied in both settings when teacher and therapist work together.

Working memory

The phonological component of the working memory is known to be deficient in readers with the severe, complex and persistent written language difficulties known as dyslexia, and to contribute to the spoken language difficulties referred to above. These relationships, as well as the nature of working memory, are well described by Gathercole and Baddeley (1993) but it is necessary to explain what is meant by 'working memory' here, to give a background to some of the activities recommended later for children with persistent phonological weaknesses. The working memory, previously known as the short-term memory, is concerned with the temporary maintenance of information. It comprises two main sub-systems: one concerned with visual material, the other with phonological material. The latter, termed the articulatory loop, consists of a phonological store in which phonological information is encoded, and an articulatory rehearsal process whereby the information is re-played or refreshed. Thus it seems that when verbal material – for example, a pair of words – is heard, it is processed and held briefly in the articulatory loop until some task – in this example, a rhyming judgement – has been carried out. The articulatory component of working memory may not operate efficiently for a number of reasons, and here we suggest two possible explanations:

1. Despite adequate hearing acuity, individuals may not set up stable representations in the phonological store. That is, they do not set up a clear enough memory trace, so judgements are made on the basis of 'fuzzy' impressions.
2. The articulatory rehearsal mechanism may be unable to hold two items simultaneously. In other words, the memory trace fades too quickly so that, in effect, the first word has been lost before the second one can be compared with it.

These are complex ideas, and, as far as young children are concerned, the possibility of enhancing memory skills for the purposes of raising phonological awareness has not been fully explored. The suggestions which we make later in this chapter have been trialled, by us, both with children demonstrating poor rhyming skills, and those with spoken language difficulties. The outcome of our trials was favourable, indicating that working memory can be improved in young children to facilitate phonological judgements.

> Where structured opportunities are routinely provided for young children to develop and practise their phonological skills it becomes relatively straightforward to check each child's phonological awareness in the context of overall development. The potential benefit of this type of approach is well illustrated by this comment about a child in her class from a nursery teacher, who had used phonological routines for the first time:
>
> > 'This has given me an insight … I now realise that there are problems which aren't at all obvious. J seems very bright but she may have problems which we would never otherwise have recognised.'

Checking out each child

Many teachers use checklists as a quick and effective means of recording individual children's responses during group activities, and many construct their own checklists for a whole variety of skills. When phonological awareness is included on these checklists, this area of pre-literacy development is unlikely to be neglected. Most teachers prefer to design their own format for recording progress, but we suggest that phonological skills are monitored according to the broad categories listed below. These can then be checked by reference to children's performance on the activities suggested in Chapter 2. We have reproduced the names of those activities here, but reference should be made to the original descriptions for details of what each game involves. This list is not intended to be exhaustive but it should provide a working framework to support the process of checking on each child's phonological skills:

- Attending to words – as demonstrated in *If-I-Say-Your-Name* (Activity 1, page 19)
- Syllabification – for example, *What did you eat today?* (Activity 2, page 20)
- Rhyme awareness – for example, *Favourite Foods* (Activity 4, page 22)
- Rhyme judgement – as in *Odd-One-Out* (Activity 5, page 24)
- Rhyme production – as demonstrated in *The Picnic Game* (Activity 6, page 26)

Teachers can informally assess each child, with regard to general maturity, attention and listening skills, and spoken language development. Additionally, they can consider the child's individual approach to learning, and home background factors. By reference to the picture which emerges from this information, teachers will be able to gauge how much further practice is needed before assuming a real difficulty with any of the skills indicated by the categories. This process of building up and learning from individual profiles of children's abilities and learning characteristics is illustrated in the case studies below.

A continuous process of checking, via this framework, can be achieved through a range of classroom activities, not just those specifically targeting phonological awareness. For example, opportunities to check on children's listening skills may arise, quite incidentally, when they are waiting to hear their names at registration. At other times, children might spontaneously comment on words that rhyme, or might generate rhymes for themselves. These informal demonstrations can be recorded on the checklist.

We have explained that it is important to take account of a number of factors which may impact on a child's ability to benefit from phonological activities, particularly when planning further input for individual children. The examples below illustrate this by looking at children's profiles in terms of their phonological awareness within the context of their more general progress.

Phonological progress in children: case studies

Sarah – a 'bright' and chatty child

Sarah is described by her teacher as a bright and chatty little girl who contributes enthusiastically to class discussions. She is well stimulated, has a wide vocabulary and gives no cause for concern within the nursery. Along with her peers she participates in a programme of phonological activities which are a daily feature of her nursery class. Her teacher uses a checklist to record individual children's responses, and was surprised to find that Sarah responded to rhyming activities either by opting out or by linking words according to their meaning rather than to their sound.

For example, when playing *The Picnic Game* Sarah completed the couplet in the following way:

> Riskits, tiskits, miskits, wiskits
> Shall we have some chocolate *cake*!

Her teacher has taken this discrepancy seriously, recognising a mismatch between Sarah's usual learning capabilities and her performance on phonologically based tasks. Sarah has been given some specific help in the form of a series of focused activities, similar to those described at the end of this chapter.

Jenny – making good progress

Jenny is in the same nursery class as Sarah, and is similarly eager to participate. She too is talkative, outgoing and is an active member of the class. Given her overall pattern of development the teacher did not expect her to have any difficulty with the phonological tasks. Her responses to these activities confirmed the teacher's opinion: Jenny was as comfortable categorising words on the basis of their shared sounds as on their linked meanings. For example, she was confident in categorising *cat* along with *dog* and *mouse*, in one context, and then for rhyming games, recognised that *cat*, *hat*, and *mat* share a common feature. In summary, Jenny seemed to acquire good phonological awareness quite effortlessly.

Jonathan – a child with 'unexpectedly' good phonological awareness

Jonathan is a quiet child. He rarely volunteers information, but is happy to answer direct questions and usually responds appropriately. The teacher knew that he did not have a particularly rich language experience and, in the past, has described him as an average child but not especially bright. Her individual records of his performance show that he was actually exceptionally good at phonological training routines. For example, after very little practice he began to generate rhymes for himself and thoroughly enjoyed rhyming word-play.

The profiles kept for the three children described above show that some of the usual indicators of general learning ability do not necessarily reveal a child's potential for developing phonological skills. In other words we should not assume that a child's usual facility for learning will necessarily apply to the acquisition of phonological skills. It is worth restating a point made earlier: **we won't know whether children have these phonological skills unless we ask them to demonstrate them.**

By looking at some different patterns of development we can consider other information we might gather about children and how this might guide our approaches for tackling their phonological difficulties.

Vanessa – a child with limited language experience

Vanessa is 4 years old and the eldest of five children. She presents as a chatty, enthusiastic member of the class. If anything, she can be a little too keen and is difficult to engage, preferring to direct operations herself. Vanessa's nursery teacher is aware that the child's mother struggles to cope alone, and each of her children is from time to time sent to stay with other family members. The family are loving and supportive but the type of word-play which would promote phonological awareness is not a priority, given the family circumstances. Vanessa's speech sound system is a little delayed, making her speech understandable but very much like that of a younger child: this mild delay has not been considered serious enough to warrant referral to speech and language therapy. Vanessa has always been very keen to respond during routine phonological tasks but, in the past, sometimes seemed to miss the point of the activity, trying to draw attention to factors other than the sounds in words.

For example: Vanessa was asked to complete the following item in the *Favourite Foods* game:

> *Teacher* 'Polly Parrot likes a …?'
> *Vanessa* 'When I stayed with auntie we went to the zoo, we saw a parrot, and he liked grapes …'

The teacher was unsure about Vanessa's responses to phonological tasks, and it was difficult to investigate these fully, within the group. So she arranged for a volunteer classroom helper to give Vanessa some individual attention, working on some of the games the teacher was carrying out with the whole class. The volunteer noticed how quickly Vanessa grasped the idea of attending to sounds within words and described her as 'learning it as we go along'. This child has only mild phonological processing difficulties, but with the advantage of early recognition, it was possible to promote her awareness of the sound structure of words before she started to learn to read.

Kylie – a child with generally delayed development

Kylie is different again. She is generally delayed in most skills, with poor concentration and learning difficulties in most areas. As her teacher might have expected, she performed poorly on games and tasks featuring phonological skills. The teacher has considered Kylie's attempts at the phonological tasks in the light of her overall learning ability and progress in the nursery so far. Given that the teacher would have expected most 4-year-olds to have been able to cope with the tasks she is not surprised that Kylie, whose overall performance is more like that of a 3-year-old, has struggled with them. On reflection the teacher thinks it likely that Kylie's attention and concentration levels are not mature enough for her to focus sufficiently well on the tasks to make judgements about the sounds in words. Although Kylie's phonological awareness is certainly delayed it is clearly not yet appropriate to focus on it specifically. The teacher's priority for this child then is to promote more mature attention and general listening skills.

Christopher – a child with severe speech difficulties

Christopher is a child with a severe and persistent spoken language difficulty. His speech sound system is so poorly developed that his speech is extremely difficult to understand without a context. There is a strong family history of both spoken and written language difficulties, some of which have persisted into adulthood in other family members. Apart from his obvious language problems Christopher is making extremely good progress and is regarded as a very bright little boy. His teacher has been checking the phonological awareness of the whole class but Christopher's spoken language problem, along with the family history, alerted her to the possibility that he may have underlying phonological processing difficulties. He has had great difficulty with the games and tasks whether they were presented in a group or individually. His teacher continues to liaise with Christopher's regular speech and language therapist, and together they have explored the links between his speech problem and his difficulties with making judgements about the sounds in words. They found some of the games and tasks that the therapist had been carrying out with Christopher were simpler forms of some of those that the teacher had been trying with him. The teacher has been able to reinforce some of these activities and adapted others to use in the classroom, both with Christopher and with other children. The therapist, in turn, has gained a greater insight into the potential influence of her input on a range of phonological skills. Although specifically concerned with trying to develop Christopher's speech sound system she has become aware of the importance of considering the impact her work can have on a child's pre-literacy skills.

How to help children with poor phonological abilities

Generally speaking, there are two main approaches to working with children who struggle with phonological activities. We can simply provide more opportunities to practise the tasks they find difficult. Alternatively, tasks can be broken down into simpler steps by focusing on the component skills.

Research has not yet established which of these two approaches might be the more effective, or which children might respond to which approach although we have already suggested that further practice might be effective in some cases, and we have given examples to illustrate this. In the absence of *conclusive* evidence, however, an eclectic approach is recommended. The activities suggested in Chapter 2 can simply be repeated, either in their current form or adapted to suit a new application or game, to fit in with any part of the child's daily routine, at school or at home, for example *The Picnic Game* can be adapted for a visit to the farm:

> Habit, tabbit, mabbit, cabbit
> In this hutch we'll see a ...

or it can be integrated into the daily routine

> Thinner, pinner, winner, spinner
> Now let's go and have our dinner

Addressing the component skills

By looking at the profiles of individual children we have already begun to consider why it is that some children may not develop sufficient phonological awareness to support early reading and writing, despite the opportunity to take part in routine phonological activities. When continued practice does not produce any significant improvement in a child's ability in this area we should consider targeting component skills and working on the underlying problem. Where possible, working collaboratively with the child's speech and language therapist will provide the most effective approach for those whose problems also affect spoken language development. However, we can also help those children who do not have speech and language therapy to build up the skills they need to develop phonological awareness.

General principles

In discussing why it is that, for some children, phonological awareness is strongly resistant to training, we raised the possibility that phonological processing difficulties could be implicated. Earlier we suggested that, even where poor phonological processing does not adversely affect spoken language to the extent of requiring speech and language therapy, certain processes – for example, those impacting on working memory – may be under-functioning (Gathercole and Baddeley, 1993). To address those difficulties some level of one-to-one attention is necessary: in the case of Vanessa, a volunteer was engaged to provide support under the teacher's guidance. Individual help provides opportunities for the child to attend closely; to hear clearly, and to ask for repetitions. Additionally, adults working with the child can respond to clues revealing particular difficulties, and develop the teaching approach in accordance with those difficulties. For example, memory difficulties often become quite apparent in a one-to-one setting when children ask for repetitions of target words; they misremember words, or they simply forget what has been said to them. Young children can acquire strategies for promoting memory efficiency, or, at least, for compensating for a poor auditory memory.

Memory techniques – 'Look, listen and remember'

Collect, from the classroom, pictures of objects. Say to the child:

> 'I want to see how good you are at remembering. I'm going to say some words and you'll say them after me. At first it'll be quite easy because you'll have some pictures to remind you. Now, listen and look …
> *car … book*
> Now you …
> You were very good at that, so now I'm going to make it more difficult. I'm going to put one of the pictures down so that you can't see it and you've got to remember the word I say and just think about the picture that goes with the word. Are you ready?'

- Then repeat the words, re-presenting the pictures, one of which will be face down.
- Introduce a new pair of words, revealing the picture of only one.
- Increase the complexity of the game, by using three words and pictures, eventually concealing two pictures.
- Try playing the game without any pictures or visual prompts, but ask the child to imagine pictures to remember what was said.
- At all levels, make the repetition of the words *in sequence*, a goal of the game.

Syllable counting – sorting the toys

Collect six toys from the classroom, two each representing two-, three- and four-syllable words. Label three boxes, *1*, *2* and *3*. Also have, to hand, coloured counters.

> *shoe, car, key* (Note: use words ending in vowel sounds only, for one-syllable words)
> *pencil, cushion, jig-saw*
> *telephone, elephant, stickle-bricks*

Say to the child:

> 'We're going to tidy these things away. But first we've got to say the words that go with them. Ready … *chair … cushion … elephant* [and so on, until all the objects have been named]. Now we're going to tap the beats in the words … [name the objects and tap the syllables]. You tap the beats and I'll put out counters to show how many beats there are in each word [as the child taps each syllable, push forward one counter]. So, how many beats are there in *cushion*? [Count the counters together.] That's right, there are two. Let's put the cushion in the box marked with a '2' …'

Once children have mastered these component skills they should be better prepared to tackle the phonological games which are part of the classroom routine.

The last two chapters have described the ways in which phonological awareness develops in most children and how it can be promoted in young pre-readers. We have also suggested ways in which those children with poorly developed phonological skills may be identified and given appropriate help at an early stage.

A large body of conclusive research, notably that by Bryant and Bradley (1985) shows a clear relationship between early phonological skills and the development of reading and spelling. Those children who as pre-readers become aware of rhyme, understand that spoken language can be broken into segments of sound and enjoy active word-play will be better prepared apprentice readers-spellers. Chapter 4 will focus on how children use their phonological foundation skills to make a start on reading and spelling.

Sound Patterns and Spelling Patterns

In Chapters 2 and 3 we looked at possible approaches to promoting phonological awareness in young children before they start learning to read, and also to identifying pre-readers who are struggling to acquire phonological skills. You will recognise three broad groups of children emerging from this process:

- those who appear to develop good phonological awareness effortlessly;
- those who seem to need some specific extra help, but go on to acquire these skills;
- those who, despite focused help, still find phonological tasks difficult but are otherwise ready to start reading.

This chapter will consider the further progress of children in the first two groups, that is, those who are ready to make the connections between letter-patterns and segments of spoken words. Children in the third group are likely to find these connections difficult to make, and their problems are the focus of Chapter 5.

Independent literacy – the goal of learning to read and spell

The goal of teaching children to read and write is independent literacy. That is, readers need the strategies to tackle previously unseen words to extract meaning, and, as writers, they must have the techniques to encode words which, previously, they have only heard. They can then engage fully with written language in all its forms. Through this wider experience the individual progresses to the higher literacy skills which we associate with academic and personal achievement.

> Children who begin learning about written language after practice in segmenting spoken words and attending to the structural features of speech will more easily understand how the alphabet encodes spoken words. They are also ready to build strategies which they will then call upon selectively as the demands on their literacy skills increase.

We should perhaps take stock of the knowledge which children with good phonological awareness bring to the task of learning to read.

Grammar and syntax

By the time most 5-year-olds start to learn to read, their spoken language skills, although not fully developed, are quite advanced so that they can communicate effectively. But most of their language 'knowledge' is implicit.

For example:

Tom [aged 3]: I teached my mouses to do tricks

Tom has clearly not copied, or parroted this statement. He has constructed it, using his knowledge of his native grammar. English grammar dictates that to make a verb refer to the past, we usually add an /id/, /d/ or /t/ sound; also if we want to make some classes of words plural, we add /iz/. Tom would also be aware that the meanings of utterances are partly conveyed by their structure (the syntax), so he would know the difference between

The tiger bit the giraffe

and

The giraffe bit the tiger

But it is most unlikely that he could comment on any of these features.

Metalinguistic knowledge

Additionally, as we have already seen in Chapters 1 and 2, most pre-readers will reflect on language as an object of study in its own right, particularly if their early experience has included rhymes and other language routines. That is, they have some metalinguistic awareness. Such competence is obviously linked to cognitive maturity, and so only children whose general development is age-appropriate will be capable of this level of functioning. Even so, the 5-year-old's capacity for reflection on language itself is fragile, and, as teachers, we should take this into account when asking children about language and linguistic concepts.

For example, words and the ideas they stand for can easily become confused in a child's reasoning:

Teacher: Which word is longer, 'snake' or 'caterpillar'?
Sam [aged 5]: 'Snake' … I know, 'cos I saw a snake on the telly, and it was really, really long and it was killing this rabbit, and …

To overcome this confusion teachers can include some 'props' in the form of written-down words when asking children to judge which of two words is the longer. At the same time, drawing attention to phonological structure by splitting spoken words into syllables and beating out the syllables will reinforce the message, and re-affirm that the task in hand is concerned with thinking about the words themselves.

Perception of spoken language and the influence of written language knowledge

Once children begin to make observations on the structure of spoken language we become aware that some of their perceptions of words and utterances are different to those of written language users. This is because familiarity with the written form actually changes the way we perceive the structural features of language.

For example, what Steven Pinker calls 'the seamlessness of speech' (Pinker, 1994), by which he means that words melt fluidly into pre-ceding and succeeding words, makes it easier for us to understand utterances, but makes it very difficult for language users to note word boundaries. For young children who have not yet had the experience of linking single written words with spoken equivalents it may require a lot of practice to isolate specified single words from:

I wanna drinka milk

Furthermore the way a word is usually pronounced, in continuous speech, may not provide a good model for spelling it. Try saying the following words. At the same time consider how your usual pronunciation differs from that suggested by the spelling:

Goodbye (do you hear the /d/?)
Must be (mussbe)
Give me (gimme)

These examples illustrate an effect known as coarticulation. This occurs when speech sounds, produced in rapid succession, become contaminated with features of one another. Coarticulation underlies some of the misspellings of young children and will be revisited in a later section of this book. Meanwhile we need to understand how young children 'hear' (perceive) utterances, so that we do not assume a knowledge of language which actually derives, to some consider-able extent, from the experience of reading and writing.

Although reading and writing go on to affect the way we perceive spoken language, a pre-reading awareness of language, particularly reflecting on its sound-structure, prepares apprentice readers for 'cracking the alphabetic code'. Later, a reciprocal relationship emerges whereby phonological awareness and reading/spelling be-come mutually facilitative – reading, and particularly spelling, ability seem to enhance phonological awareness; phonological awareness promotes reading and spelling. We will show how this process can be exploited in the teaching of reading and spelling in the next section.

First, though, we recognise that other 'within-child' factors, such as the ability to listen attentively together with age-appropriate spoken language and cognitive competence, will clearly affect progress and should be noted during the routine monitoring of children's approach to literacy-related tasks.

> Provided children's performance in most areas is age-appropriate, it is reasonable to expect that, on school entry, they will have an awareness of language as an object of study in its own right.

Following on from this, they should be sensitive to the sound-structure of words at the syllable level and at the onset–rime level. These are the language skills which most children bring to the task of learning to read and spell. On the other hand, very few children will develop the skills into usable strategies without explicit teaching.

The role of teaching in consolidating the skills and developing the strategies

In this chapter we are focusing on children whose awareness of phonological segments is well established. But it is worth restating that, whatever teachers may believe about the pre-school experience of individual children, they should check, for themselves, that beginning readers have mastered pre-reading skills, such as the ability to judge and generate rhymes. This is advised partly because nursery education is variable in quantity and quality, but it is particularly in recognition of the fact that some children are now entering mainstream as 4-year-olds and so developmentally, may not be ready for the decoding activities which are essential to reading. The activities suggested in Chapter 2, in connection with pre-schoolers, can be developed for use with pre-readers in the Reception class, but teachers may want to check on vocabulary to exclude words which, although rhyming, are spelt differently, for example, *fox/socks*.

From the outset, teachers must be aware of the direction in which apprentice reader–writers should be moving so that, at any point, they can build in sign-posts to later developments:

> Tim, aged 6, is writing about his new pet rabbit, Rhubarb. He asks his teacher to put the rabbit's name in his spelling dictionary. Instead of simply writing the name in Tim's dictionary, she takes the opportunity to syllabify the word, **and** to point out the silent letter, explaining that some words have letters which we don't hear. But she assures Tim that he will learn more about these silent letters later on.

Logographic strategies

The initial stages of learning to read are usually concerned with building up a sight vocabulary, a bank or lexicon of word shapes associated with meaning (see Chapter 1). It is important to realise that many young children link the whole shape directly with meaning, before they link it with the corresponding word.

> *Teacher* (presenting a word-card on which is printed a child's name): Read this to me, please.
> *Jenny*: It's me.
> *Teacher*: No, that's not quite right. It says 'Jenny'.
> *Jenny*: That's what I said.

One of the earliest connections which they must make is that the shape represents a word, not just an idea. In the previous section we proposed that teachers might use flash-cards to reinforce the notion of 'longer' and 'shorter' words, linking the visually apparent difference between written-down words with the longer- or shorter-sounding words. Using the same exercise we can highlight the difference between ideas and words.

For example, flash-cards are displayed in most early years classrooms: *table* attached to teacher's table, *window* to the window, and so on. Research evidence that demonstrated children's inability to note changes in commercial logos (Ehri, 1987) has been interpreted as suggesting that pre-reading children 'read' the environmental object, not the print that labels it. So, it seems, these children are largely unaware of what is printed on classroom labels. Consequently, these contribute little to children's learning *unless* they are encouraged to focus on the words themselves.

- Try swapping the labels around while the children are out of the classroom, then invite them to see what's different.

Inevitably, beginning readers will spot the difference first so the activity will have to be controlled to give the less-advanced children a chance.

- Ask all the children to draw a classroom object that has the wrong label attached.
- This game can be developed by substituting new labels – *floor* for *door*; *cable* for *table*, followed by discussion about what is different.

A common starting point for reading is word identification or 'Look-and-Say'. This has a place for establishing a sight-word vocabulary and for addressing some of the basic concepts necessary for the business of reading, such as the left–right direction of written language and, as we have seen, for making the leap from idea to word. Even at this stage children can be encouraged to reflect on the phonological structure of the words in their sight-vocabulary, perhaps by drawing their attention to the initial sounds and by pointing out that these are represented by the same letter. In this case, it cannot be emphasised too strongly that the words which are being linked must start with the same sound and not just the same letter.

For example, the words 'Trish' and 'Tom' do not sound the same at the beginning, through a 5-year-old's ears! This is because they do not have the same onset – *Trish* starts with /tr/; *Tom* starts with /t/.

As we have seen, the average 5-year-old will probably be able to break into a syllable at the onset–rime level, but further analysis depends on well-established literacy skills.

Introducing alphabetic strategies through the use of analogies

In many classrooms teachers introduce single letters and their sound-equivalents, alongside activities for building a sight-vocabulary. Phonic activities work well with most children for initial sounds and their corresponding letters. Beyond this, the reader must be able to break into the word at the level of single letters or letters representing single phonemes.

> C...A...T for /c/.../a/.../t/
> F...I...S...H for /f/.../i/.../sh/
> O...U...G...H...T for /ough/.../t/

This is notoriously difficult to do, particularly as there are many more phonemes in the language than there are letters with which to represent them. We must assume that apprentice readers are using a range of strategies to arrive at accurate pronunciations and meaningful words.

One of these strategies involves the use of analogies: the reader who is able to recognise the rhyming quality of two or more words may be primed for reading unknown words on the basis of an orthographic similarity to a word in the sight-vocabulary.

For example: Mark will undoubtedly be able to read his name. This could give him access to *dark, park, lark, bark* ... provided he also knows some initial sound-letters.

Although children might spontaneously use analogies to support their early reading and spelling, they can also be taught how to make the link, so it is essential for teachers to understand the basis of this skill and techniques for promoting it in beginning readers.

Language knowledge and literacy skills
We know, from the work of linguists studying the structure of spoken language (for example, Fudge, 1969) that there are good acoustic reasons why it is relatively easy to break into words at the syllable level. Thereafter, the vowel-sound in a syllable is highly salient to speakers–hearers, and, for them, the syllable divides into the sounds which come before the vowel (the onset) and those which include and come after it (the rime). So the syllable is accessible to the speaker–hearer at the onset–rime level. Beyond that it is quite difficult for individuals to analyse the syllable any further although fluent readers believe they can break it down into individual sounds. In

fact, what we have access to is an approximation to those sounds which is mediated by our knowledge of spelling: our real 'knowledge' about individual phonemes is restricted to an awareness of the contrasts between words, for example, those which vary by only one phoneme as in *tip* and *pip*.

It is unlikely that beginning readers will spontaneously analyse syllables into component sounds (or the sounds represented by single graphemes), but their sensitivity to rhyme and alliteration suggests they can analyse the syllable at the onset–rime level. These assertions about syllable-structure have been fully developed by Rebecca Treiman (Treiman, 1985). Elsewhere, Usha Goswami (1995) has shown how children can and do make use of this linguistic knowledge when, recognising visual patterns in new words, they extend their knowledge of the sound of those patterns so that they arrive at pronunciations for the unknown words.

We should be aware that this process involves, not just phonological awareness, but a cognitive strategy known as analogy. This strategy involves, firstly, recognising the similarity between two things, one of which is familiar and the other, unfamiliar – in this case, we are talking about two words. The second part of the analogy process involves taking our knowledge about the familiar item and using it to understand the unfamiliar item, at the same time being able to make deductions about the point of difference between the two items. While its application to reading and spelling can be taught as research has shown (Marsh *et al.*, 1981), it is dependent on a certain level of maturity of thinking which allows children to reflect, simultaneously, on two or more aspects of a problem.

As a strategy 'Reading by analogy' has many advantages:

- it makes use of the child's existing knowledge of sight-words
- it makes use of a tendency known to characterise fluent readers as well as beginners
- it reduces memory loading
- it enables the reader to attempt words which could not be accessed by single letter-to-sound conversions.

Making use of children's existing bank of sight-words

In a series of experiments Usha Goswami demonstrated that young children make spontaneous use of analogies to generalise from words which they already know by sight in order to read new words (Goswami, 1995). That is, they recognise spelling patterns within words, attach a pronunciation to that pattern and try the pronunciation within the new word. Goswami emphasised that the process nearly always operates at the onset–rime level, so that young readers are much more likely, for example, to attempt the word *mouse* by addressing *-ouse* than *mou-*.

Reading by analogy is used by fluent readers, not just beginners
Cognitive psychologists have attempted to build up models of the reading process for computer simulations (for example, see Ellis, 1984). They hypothesise that fluent, effective readers, in attempting to decode words which they have not previously seen, focus on the largest visual pattern that they recognise. Just as described in connection with beginning readers, the fluent reader then attaches a pronunciation. Consider the selection of words below:

tpozh – this would be rejected, out-of-hand, because it comprises letter combinations which are not allowed in English.

blem – it is unlikely that this would be constructed, one letter-to-sound at a time. Instead, *bl* is a frequently-encountered consonant blend, *-em* is often read in *them*. The combination, *-lem*, is known from *lemon* but, breaking into the onset as it would, this will not serve as a cue in this context.

gairmank – initially, this is split into component syllables. The first syllable, *gair-*, is divided into the onset, *g*, then the rime, *-air*, which, in this case, contains no consonant sound. The rime is instantly recognisable as a word in its own right and from many everyday words in English, *chair, stair, pair*. The second syllable is then processed, onset, *m-*, and rime, *-ank*, which, of course, produces a different and much more acceptable pronunciation than if '*man*' had been extracted for decoding. Again this is a familiar pattern in the words *thank, drank, sank*.

Reading by analogy reduces cognitive loading
Let's consider again one of the nonsense words from the previous section, *blem*. We have already seen that, as fluent readers, our spontaneous approach to this would *not* be one letter, one sound at a time, '*buh-luh-e-muh*'. One reason for this is that separating the letters in this way and linking them with their most usual sounds leads to distortion when the schwa sound *uh* is produced. Secondly, it requires some feat of memory to decode and hold onto each separate sound, and finally to blend them in the correct sequence, so to access a pronunciation. We are all familiar with the range of errors – missequenced sounds, omitted sounds, perseverated sounds – which result from one-letter, one-sound decoding.

Reading by analogy gives access to a wide range of spelling patterns
As Goswami (1996b) points out, there is a much greater spelling-to-sound consistency in the English orthography at the onset–rime level than at the level of single letters. Consider the spelling pattern *-ought*. Once this is linked with a pronunciation that sound is reproduced in many words, *bought; brought; fought; thought*, and so on. While we accept that this does not meet every criticism of English spelling, for example, the sound represented by *ought* can also be spelt -ORT, or -AUGHT, the reader has much more chance of accessing the word through a knowledge of the spelling pattern than by sounding out the individual letters, O...U...G...H...T.

Activities to promote the use of analogies

1. A technique which is increasingly being favoured by teachers as a new approach to phonics involves providing the spelling of the rime of a one-syllable word, and asking children to make new words by adding the onsets. For example, the simplest approach is to provide a complete, known word:

   in
   then add, *b, t, w, p*
   (keeping similar-sounding phonemes separate)
   then, *ch, sh, th*
   then, *sp, tw, gr*

   The blending of onset and rime is most effective if you *don't* emphasise the separate sound of the onset as you add it, as in 'buh-in'. It should be sufficient to say the complete word with a slight delay on the first sound. Other examples of rimes which are also complete words are:

   it; at; am; on; an; and; all; ill

   Again, to avoid confusion introduce separately syllables which have the same vowels or similar final consonants.
   Once this procedure has been established with a number of known words, introduce rimes which are not known words. For example:

   -et; -ip; -ell ; -ot; -en.

2. Make word jigsaws as suggested below. The children cut out the jigsaw pattern and their teacher pronounces the rime of the words. Children identify which rime they heard the teacher say. They mix and match the onsets, identifying any nonsense words.

Word Jigsaws		
big	wet	fall
dog	lip	mug
man	pill	top

The role of spelling in early reading

While the activity described in the previous section could not be called spelling (because spelling is essentially the encoding of spoken words) it does involve generating new words for reading. In that sense, it begins to introduce the notion that written words are constructed. They do not, as many young children seem to think, have an impenetrable structure which readers have to memorise. Moreover, words which the children have created can be read by another person. These are aspects of written language which beginning reader–writers gradually come to understand.

Once children start to write they will have to use an alphabetic strategy unless an adult is going to supply every new word for them. Opinions divide on the best way of promoting children's writing – should children be encouraged to attempt the spelling of new words for themselves, or should they be given the correct spelling? In trying to spell words by letter-to-sound correspondence young writers will inevitably produce many unconventional spellings and clearly they must eventually abandon their strictly phonetic attempts in favour of the conventional versions. On the other hand, if they are only allowed to write words for which they have models their experience of attending closely to the phonological structure will be severely restricted. Whichever approach is adopted we should remember that, in the early stages, children may read words they cannot spell and spell words they are unable to read. So it is always worth asking children to read back their own stories (once they have had time to forget what they wrote!).

Traditional phonic approaches emphasise a 'bottom-up' approach. This teaches the sounds of individual letters which the reader must then blend into words. Nowadays it is widely regarded as mechanistic, tedious to teach and often unsuccessful. Variations on the theme are called 'New Phonics'. These take a new look at the old system and teach patterns larger than the single letter, usually the pattern representing the rime of a syllable. This type of approach certainly has the potential to be more successful for the reasons given earlier. Whether it is more effective depends on how it is taught.

Making the most of commercial resources or schemes

Some new reading schemes include phonological training. Commercial phonological training activities are usually concerned with:
- spellings of onsets and rimes
- demonstrating how analogies work.

Clearly the effectiveness of commercial resources is extended when the underlying message is reinforced by supportive teaching.

> Becoming an independent reader and writer (speller) is largely a matter of 'cracking the alphabetic code'.

When readers can unlock meaning from printed words by attaching sounds to letters, thereby accessing spoken words, they can go on to practise this skill until it becomes automatic. Similarly, by means of the same basic skill, they can represent words which they hear with consistent and logical spelling patterns. Further reading consolidates more complex spellings and other orthographic knowledge. Reading and spelling provide another window on language as an object of study, and so phonological skills are also enhanced.

Ongoing use of phonological strategies

For example, readers, unlike non-readers, are able to manipulate phonemes:

'Say *string* without the *rrrrr*';

Secret language codes, traditionally associated with children's games, as in Pig Latin:

'Put the first sound of *pig* at the end and add *ay*.' (*igpay*)

While these activities are no more than 'tricks' made up by linguists to measure phonological skills they illustrate strategies which *are* used by fluent readers to pronounce, and particularly to spell, new words. For spelling, we segment novel words which we hear into sound patterns, individual sounds if necessary. We then think about how these sounds are usually spelt and here our 'orthographic' knowledge dictates different spellings for different positions in a word.

Example:

We know that *ghikne* could not spell *fine* , even though

GH spells /f/ in *enough*

KN spells /n/ in *know*

These representations are not allowable in these word-positions.

So alphabetic knowledge together with orthographic knowledge, largely gained through the experience of reading and writing, allows us to attempt recognisable – and often, conventional – spellings.

In Chapter 6 we will consider how poor phonological awareness and its cumulative impact on reading, spelling and study skills affect secondary pupils. But in the next chapter we will consider how to help those children who are unable to progress beyond a basic level of reading and spelling because their sensitivity to the sound-structure of language is under-developed.

Chapter 5

Early Reading and Spelling Problems: The Phonological Aspects

In Chapter 4 we outlined techniques and approaches for promoting reading and spelling in pupils who, on school entry, are ready to make the connections between alphabetic letters and speech sounds. These are the pupils with good phonological awareness. The present chapter focuses on children whose written language development, during the first three years of schooling, is causing concern. In particular, it looks at:

- the features of the children's reading and spelling which suggest that the origins of the difficulties are principally in the phonological domain;
- the range of difficulties under the phonological 'umbrella', and the reading and spelling problems which they create;
- where to start and what to do;
- how a teaching-approach can be extended by contributions from other professionals.

Where activities to promote sensitivity to the sound-structure of words are an ongoing feature of the day-to-day routine, children who might simply need a bit of extra practice or encouragement are well provided for. Additionally, careful observation will reveal which children are not responding appropriately to, for example, rhyming games. These children may also be struggling with certain aspects of written language.

Children with phonological difficulties can often make a promising start on reading. They are keen and build up a fund of sight-words quite easily, making good use of context clues. Problems start to become apparent when, unlike their peers, these readers don't seem able to attempt new words, or their attempts are restricted to sounding out the first letter only.

While our current concern is with the phonological aspects of reading problems we fully recognise that there are many other skill-areas which might be failing a young reader. For example, children's ability to control eye-movements so that they can track smoothly across lines of print might need to be checked, also poor pencil-grip and control, easily detected while a child is writing, can interfere with progress which in turn limits experience and further opportunity to learn. **In other words, attention to phonological factors should supplement, not replace, the monitoring of other literacy-related skills.**

Moving on from look-and-say: what might be the problem?

Reading-progress, particularly the transition from early word-by-word decoding to fluent effective reading, is often lightly described when we say that children 'just take off'. In fact, they don't take off, they cotton on – or most children do. They cotton on to, or make, the links between the segments of sound that they hear and the letters and letter-patterns that they see in written words, particularly when written language instruction in the classroom emphasises this approach. But a minority of children fail to make the links and we gradually become aware that a gap is opening up between them and their peers.

From 'look-and-say': what might develop?

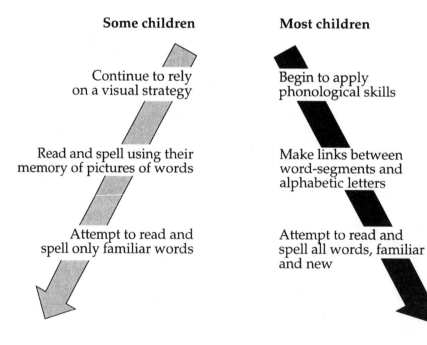

Some children	Most children
Continue to rely on a visual strategy	Begin to apply phonological skills
Read and spell using their memory of pictures of words	Make links between word-segments and alphabetic letters
Attempt to read and spell only familiar words	Attempt to read and spell all words, familiar and new

A closer look at these children, who are often coping quite adequately in other areas of learning, reveals a number of specific indicators which show that they have failed to grasp the principles underlying the alphabetic code:

- They persist in their use of whole-word (logographic) strategies for reading, despite encouragement to use letter–sound links. This often involves volunteering a word which is appropriate to the context, but the sound of which could not be represented by the written form.
- They are reluctant to attempt new words. Alternatively, they respond with, 'I don't know that word' or otherwise clearly imply that, in their understanding, readers can only read words they have met previously.
- They produce free writing which is very restricted in length, content and interest when compared with oral accounts. When asked to read back their own stories, for example, writers may be unable to read what they wrote, explaining, 'I can't *remember* what I meant'.
- Again when writing, they choose only from a spelling-vocabulary with which they are confident. This again becomes apparent as a discrepancy between their command of spoken language, particularly vocabulary, and the level of language used in writing. On its own, this is not evidence of phonological difficulties but is a technique adopted by many weak spellers. A tendency to stay with tried-and-tested vocabulary and style should be viewed in conjunction with an analysis of spelling errors.
- They make 'bizarre' spelling errors. That is, the sound, and therefore the identity of a word, cannot be deduced, via letter-to-sound correspondence, however imaginative the reader might be. For example, *gis* (*cut*) or *miH* (*mat*). Compare these with *hLept* = *helped*. This is not bizarre, but is a creative approach to spelling a word which, although recurrent in young children's literature, may be quite difficult to remember. The initial letter is correct, the final two letters could represent the last sounds in the word. The *e* is remembered as a constituent element, and many children use a letter in its capital form, *L*, to 'say its name', as in *cR-*, before they fully comprehend the function of capital letters.
- They find spelling-tests a nightmare. The child may spend many hours trying to memorise sequences of letters representing the target words, but without any phonological strategy she or he lacks a system for supporting the memory of the sequences, so the spelling is forgotten.

This 7-year-old has written, under a picture showing his 'news'. His spelling errors reveal very poor alphabetic skills.

[I sometimes help my daddy to wash the car on Saturdays. I soaked Daddy with the hose]

- They over-generalise spelling-patterns to inappropriate words. Where the teaching-approach includes linking sound-patterns with letter-patterns (phonics) children with poor phonological skills may not understand where the spelling-pattern which is currently being practised is employed. Consequently, these children use it inappropriately. For example:

The class is practising the spelling sequence *'ough'* to represent the sound segment pattern /uff/ as in *tough, rough, enough*. If a pupil cannot segment *tough* at the onset–rime juncture, represented in spelling by *t-ough* and relate the new spelling pattern to the rime, she or he will not be able to generate the spelling *rough* by analogy. Further, the pupil may apply *ough* to words which do not include a sound pattern that could be represented by this combination of letters.

Moving on from 'look-and-say': summarising the key differences

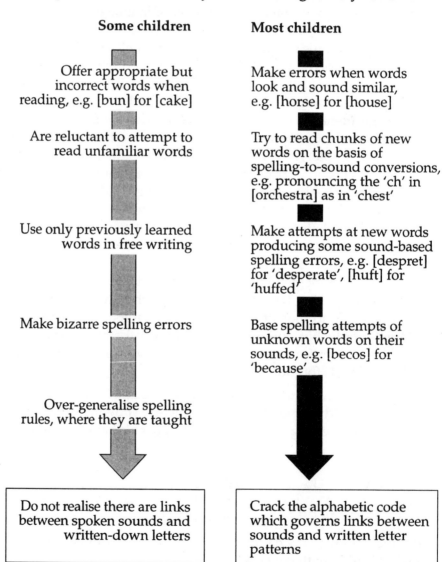

Some children	**Most children**
Offer appropriate but incorrect words when reading, e.g. [bun] for [cake]	Make errors when words look and sound similar, e.g. [horse] for [house]
Are reluctant to attempt to read unfamiliar words	Try to read chunks of new words on the basis of spelling-to-sound conversions, e.g. pronouncing the 'ch' in [orchestra] as in 'chest'
Use only previously learned words in free writing	Make attempts at new words producing some sound-based spelling errors, e.g. [despret] for 'desperate', [huft] for 'huffed'
Make bizarre spelling errors	Base spelling attempts of unknown words on their sounds, e.g. [becos] for 'because'
Over-generalise spelling rules, where they are taught	
Do not realise there are links between spoken sounds and written-down letters	Crack the alphabetic code which governs links between sounds and written letter patterns

Among the group of children identified as having phonological difficulties there will be those who are simply slower at making use of alphabetic strategies. In addition there will be those whose difficulties suggest a more fundamental problem with phonological processing. We need to distinguish between these two groups to plan appropriate intervention for them. A checklist of questions might help to start this process.

Planning the most appropriate help

Checklist

Background information

There are usually indicators in a child's early history, as well as in connection with her or his general experience, which should alert us to potential difficulties in acquiring reading and spelling. Collecting information from school files, parents, and colleagues who have taught the child will help to complete the following checklist.

Does this child have spoken language difficulties?	Yes	No
Is a speech therapist involved with her/him?	Yes	No
Does this child have a history of hearing difficulties?	Yes	No
Has she or he missed much school?	Yes	No
Are you aware of any member of this child's family who has reading problems?	Yes	No
Does she or he have a noticeable difficulty with pronouncing long words?	Yes	No
Does the child find it difficult to remember new vocabulary?	Yes	No
Did she or he struggle with pre-school phonological activities?	Yes	No
Have the child's previous class-teachers commented on problems with grasping letter-sound patterns?	Yes	No
Are the difficulties you've noted in this child unexpected in the light of her/his usual ability?	Yes	No

Interpreting the checklist

A 'yes' response to most of these questions will suggest that phonological weaknesses are at the root of a child's difficulty with making the transition from context-bound, visually-based reading and spelling strategies to the alphabetic approach that gives an apprentice reader and writer the freedom to tackle new words and new written material, quite independently. Two items – those relating to the child's attendance at school, and to general learning ability – will reveal whether other factors might account for a generally slower rate of progress. After all, if a child has not been at school to be taught, progress in all subjects will be affected. Additionally, this might suggest that the child has been unwell, and again we would expect learning to be affected by poor health. Otherwise, generalised learning difficulties may account for a child's inability to make alphabetic links and to generalise this knowledge into workable reading and spelling strategies. However, this item should not be taken to suggest that children with low general ability may not also have phonological difficulties, but it is included to raise, for consideration, the full range of factors which may impact on a child's ability to 'cotton on' to basic written language skills. The checklist is intended to be a starting point, a framework for collective observations. Further assessment of a child's phonological abilities will confirm whether these alone are responsible for the lack of progress. We suggest that the child's performance on rhyming tasks is examined, and the categories outlined in Chapter 2 could guide this process.

Skills assessment

Depending on the age of the child whose reading and spelling is causing concern, it may be necessary to modify some of the activities described in Chapter 2 to make them age-appropriate. But the principle underlying the assessment is the same: can this pupil make judgements about the sound structure of spoken words?

Activity	Has it been tried?	Right first time?	Did repetition help?
Rhyme detection			
Rhyme generation			
Rhyme judgement			

If performance on these measures of rhyming skills suggests that the child **is** aware of sound segments it will be appropriate to test the application of phonological skills to alphabetic strategies. Traditionally, one of the first measures of a child's written language ability which is taken when problems arise, is that of grapheme–phoneme correspondence. This is achieved by:

- asking the child to choose, from a display of plastic letters, the letter which says (for example) *buh*;
- asking the child what sound (for example) the letter, 'B', makes.

The extent of letter-sound knowledge must be established, but it does not reveal the whole picture. Further measures should follow to show whether the child can use the alphabetic connections in word-building and in breaking written words into components for reading. After all, a child could quite easily have learnt to pair the sound *buh* with the letter, 'B', without understanding why we link the sound and the letter, or what we do with this knowledge. We suggest that, in exploring alphabetic knowledge, it is particularly revealing to use non-words or 'made-up' words. This way, the child is forced to reflect on the letter-to-sound or sound-to-letter connections, having no previously learned visual pattern to refer to. The assessment can be conducted by using the traditional format of a spelling or reading test, using words which have been generated by analogy to real words. Alternatively, plastic letters can be used. The latter technique has distinct advantages in that it frees the child from the anxiety which may be associated with the pen-and-paper 'test', and it allows the tester to observe how the child responds to the task in very specific ways, and to manipulate the task to reveal more information.

For example, if the child is asked to construct the word *jid*, she or he may select the correct letter for the initial sound but make no further attempt. The tester might then proceed by asking the child to construct two-letter words which are in the child's spelling vocabulary, for example, *in, an, at*, and so on. Then the tester can revert to the non-word format, using, firstly, words which have been created from these rimes; and, later, words which derive from rimes such as *-id*.

The same technique can be applied to reading non-words. That is, the child will attempt a word which has been constructed from plastic letters. If this proves too difficult the tester can ask her or him to attempt part of the word – the segment which she or he could be expected to know. Having been given this strategy, the child will demonstrate later in the test whether she or he can read by analogy.

In summary, assessment should proceed from looking at a child's phonological awareness, through examining letter-sound knowledge, to investigating whether the child can use letter-sound knowledge in alphabetic strategies such as word-building and reading by analogy. We have also suggested here an approach known as 'dynamic assessment' (Spector, 1992) – in which the tester intervenes to help the child at key points and then notes whether suggested strategies are incorporated into later attempts. This is likely to be more revealing of strengths and weaknesses than a simple 'right/wrong' checklist.

The pattern of responses should begin to suggest whether a child is slowly building some alphabetic strategies, or whether there are more fundamental problems with phonological processing.

Getting there slowly
For a number of reasons some children do not 'crack the alphabetic code' as quickly as we might have expected. However, after weighing up the factors on the checklist, and looking at their responses to the assessment procedure set out above, it seems that theirs is more a case of delayed development than a persistent, underlying difficulty. Steps described later in this chapter may be particularly helpful for these children.

Persistent difficulties
In a small minority of cases pupils will not respond to reading- and spelling-based techniques because their difficulties with using alphabetic strategies have their origins in the way they process spoken language. However rich and focused their early experience with spoken

language and language games they have no access to the internal sound structure of words so the alphabetic principle, whereby letters and letter-patterns map onto speech-sounds, does not easily make sense to them. Typically, they will 'exit' from the assessment procedure described above at the first level, demonstrating poor phonological awareness. However, they may show some awareness of rhyme, only to fail when asked, for example, to change *did* to make it read, *jid*, even though it is established that they know that the initial sound is represented by the letter, J.

Children with persistent speech difficulties, particularly those receiving help from Speech and Language Therapists, are very likely to be within the group of children with poor phonological skills. The therapist will probably identify their underlying problems in order to plan therapy. This may include a kinaesthetic approach in which the child is encouraged to think about the way speech sounds are produced in the mouth. Such techniques are also known to have the potential to trigger phonological awareness, so, if therapist and teacher have the opportunity to share ideas, they can jointly arrange for reinforcement activities to feature in the child's Individual Education Plan (DfE, 1994). The same process will provide the opportunity for the therapist to discover how techniques used for teaching literacy skills can support therapy for children in this group.

Pupils with no obvious speech problems – or, at least, those whose speech is not regarded as requiring any input from Speech and Language Therapy Services – may still have underlying difficulties with phonological processing. But progressing from spoken to written language requires the child to use phonological information in a different way.

Weak foundations may support the development of spoken language but they will not support the framework for cracking the alphabetic code of written language. The most likely areas of weakness are in setting up and maintaining auditory impressions.

The nature of auditory impressions

Spoken words are transient. Once spoken, nothing remains of them except the listener's impression of what was heard. Without a mechanism to compensate for this we would never acquire any vocabulary! So the working memory, which was described more fully in Chapter 3, enables us to maintain an auditory impression of what we have just heard, for a few seconds. For most people this is long enough to make lots of decisions about this auditory information. The decisions might include consideration of whether this is a completely new word, whether it is allowable according to the sound-rules of English and what the sounds within the word are. For the children with persistent difficulties it is very likely that this mechanism is faulty. The child may not set up accurate impressions, or may not retain impressions for long enough to make any judgements.

Identifying where to start and what to do

On school entry, some children may still have a difficulty with phonological awareness tasks, despite the opportunity to take part in rhyming games and other types of word-play. Most will slowly make progress but, for a few, phonologically based tasks will remain a complete mystery. It is important to distinguish between children who have entrenched difficulties with phonological processing, and those who will respond to focused help because, when they start learning to read, these children will have different ongoing needs.

Step-by-step: gradually introducing an alphabetic approach

This approach focuses on a range of strategies which fluent written language users develop, almost 'automatically'. The intention is to introduce a series of 'making-it-easier' steps, on the assumption that, if children have struggled with phonological tasks in the past, they may have some lingering weakness in the phonological domain. So it is particularly useful for those children who are making progress, albeit more slowly than we might have expected. The expectation of these children is that they are aware that spoken words can be segmented, at the level of syllables and at the onset–rime level. Their awareness is probably not fully consolidated, so they need lots of practice in beating out syllables, listening for rhymes, judging pairs of words as rhyming or non-rhyming, starting with the same sound or not. Additionally, these children will typically find it difficult to make connections between individual sounds and the letters which represent them. Instruction, and the activities which support it, should therefore begin with looking (and listening) for patterns which are larger than individual graphemes (letters) and phonemes.

- Construct words from magnetic letters and put them together to make compound words, saying the words as you construct them.

  Example: 'foot/ball'; 'play/time'.

- Construct compound words, say the words, and take one of the components away, saying the component word as you do so. Ask pupils what is left.

  Example: 'matchstick – take away 'match'. What do we have left?'

- Note that it is not easy to develop this activity for adding and deleting syllables because the stress pattern of syllables changes when they are pronounced singly.

  Example: /carpet/ minus /car/ = /pit/, not /pet/.

Thus, this exercise cannot be presented with supporting letters, but should sometimes be used as an oral task only.

- Play rhyming games with labelled pictures. Note that, unlike games which are played with non-reading pre-schoolers, these games should feature only words where the spellings, as well as the sounds, are the same.

Example: 'Which of these words rhyme – fox, van, box?'

- Construct the rime of the syllable from plastic letters. Give pupils further letters to practise word-building by adding an onset and pronouncing it.
- Construct the whole word with plastic letters. Ask pupils to remove the onset-letter and to pronounce the pattern that remains. At first, ensure that the rime of these words is also a word in its own right.

Example: f/at; sp/it; sm/all; c/old.

Progress gradually to rimes which are not also complete words.

Example: sh/op; f/ish; st/ing.

Don't include patterns which have the same spelling but different sounds!

Example: m/ost; l/ost.

- Using the same activities to encourage analysis (breaking the words down) and synthesis (blending the components of words), introduce pairs of rimes which are minimally related.

Example: and, end.

Ask pupils to judge to which pattern you must add a sound to make words:

bend, hand, stand, mend, spend, band, and so on.

- Extend the approach to rimes which are minimally related in terms of consonant sounds.

Example: -og, ong
dog, fog, strong, log, long.

When 'Making-it-easier' isn't enough

We would hope that, by referring to the original checklist and by assessing children whose written language progress is causing concern, those who are at risk of developing severe literacy difficulties will be quickly identified. In some cases, though, children may not emerge as having serious problems until the 'making-it-easier' approach has been applied. However they are identified, it should become obvious when something more is needed. We illustrate this in the following case-study when we discuss Oliver. We describe his pattern of difficulties and their resistance to some of the 'making-it-easier' steps. We consider some of the techniques which have been used in a one-to-one setting to help Oliver.

Oliver attended a nursery where nursery rhyme activities were regularly included. He started school at four-and-a-half and his Reception teacher was surprised to discover that he had very little idea of rhyme, could not supply rhymes to a target word, nor could he say which of a selection of words rhymed. Speech therapy had apparently resolved an earlier difficulty with delayed speech development and he had been discharged from Speech and Language Therapy Services. The only persisting speech problem is a difficulty with pronouncing some long (multisyllabic) words. Bouts of hearing loss associated with catarrh are now less frequent, and Oliver rarely misses school which he loves. Oliver is a bright, able child who likes to contribute to most subjects. However, although he likes books, he made a halting start on reading, recognising many words by sight but staying firmly wedded to their visual appearance. In fact, he continues to show a remarkable facility for remembering visual patterns but does not spontaneously transfer familiar spellings to new words which share a sound. For example, he wanted to spell the word *bright* and his teacher suggested that he should think about *night* which he can spell. Oliver's attempt at *bright* then read *bnight*. More generally, as most of Oliver's peers started to use alphabetic strategies for spelling and then reading, Oliver began to lose ground quite rapidly. He doesn't understand why other children don't need to ask the teacher for the spelling of every new word, nor less what the teacher means when she asks him to try spellings for himself. He still attempts new words-for-reading by context-guessing or by supplying a word which is visually similar.

In the past, remedial attempts have focused on promoting rhyme and alliteration awareness, and on phonics. Oliver can say which words rhyme with certain tried-and-tested target words such as *cat* and *socks*. But if he is asked about a new word such as *door* he will reply that he hasn't 'done' *door*! Oliver's teacher uses onsets and rimes rather than single sounds; but even so, Oliver cannot generalise the information to go beyond the sample words which have featured in the lessons, and he usually forgets these as soon as his teacher moves onto another sound.

It has been decided that Oliver should have some one-to-one help from a Special Support assistant who is working under the combined direction of the class-teacher and the Special Needs Co-ordinator. The SSA works with Oliver in a setting where noise is reduced to the minimum and she is briefed to select from his work some key words for special attention. Oliver is working on a 'Houses and Homes' topic so the following words have been targeted: *chairs, door, wall, floor, stairs, hall.*

- The words are sorted into rhyming pairs and Oliver is helped to 'read' (say) them.
- Oliver is asked to copy a pair of words, using plastic letters.
- Oliver is encouraged/helped to discover the similarity between the sound of the words, then the spelling of the words.
- Oliver and the SSA discuss the sound of the words and say which 'chunk' they have in common. At the same time they link this to the spelling of the 'chunk'.
- Oliver writes out the pair of words, in cursive script, saying the words slowly as he writes.

Although a recurring theme of our book has been that phonological awareness must be well established *before* children can discover the key to alphabetic literacy the approach described in connection with Oliver is directed towards promoting phonological awareness *alongside* literacy skills. It is quite possible that addressing spelling in the highly-focused way we have described above, will eventually trigger phonological awareness (instead of the reverse process) when we have to accept that, for a very small group of children, phonological processes remain stubbornly resistant to training.

Sharing skills and exchanging information

There is already an established framework for liaison between teachers, specialist teachers and educational psychologists. Another potential source for discussion and development of ideas is speech and language therapists. Earlier in this book we referred to the help which this group might be able to offer. Now we should consider more specifically the skills which they bring and what they can learn about the demands of the classroom situation.

Learning to use language is probably the most complex task that we carry out, with a complicated network of associations being established. Given the complexity of the process it seems sensible to make links with other professionals whose knowledge and expertise may contribute to a better understanding of the whole process.

Speech and language therapists have training and experience in neurology, child development, analysis of speech and language processing and identification of underlying difficulties which may influence language learning. The speech and language therapist is well qualified and well placed to provide specialist advice about the processes and skills which link spoken and written language. Even more benefit, however, is derived when teacher and therapist work together in interpreting information about the child and in devising appropriate intervention. Over time they will develop a shared understanding of each other's skills and ways of working which will inform and extend their practice.

So far in this book we have looked at the role of phonological awareness in preparing young children to embark on learning to read and spell independently. We have traced the development of phonological skills in young pre-readers through to the stages where these skills are applied in making the links between speech sounds and their written-down letter equivalents. We have described the progression which most children follow, and have considered the implications of poor early phonological skills and ways in which these can be addressed. Teaching techniques to promote phonological strategies in all children have been suggested, and ways of fine-tuning some techniques for those children with more severe difficulties have been described.

In our final chapter, however, we turn to possible approaches for those students whose phonological difficulties are both severe and persistent. We may need to accept that, despite focused help, the phonological route to literacy may not be possible for some students. So, in the face of new pressures, including external examinations or the prospect of leaving full-time education, a fresh approach to tackling the difficulties created by poor literacy skills is needed.

Chapter 6

Persistent Problems and Useful Strategies

In previous chapters we have been concerned with promoting literacy skills through phonological training. We believe that if young children are encouraged to attend to the segmental nature of spoken language and are then shown, through a variety of techniques and resources, how to use our alphabet to represent those segments for spelling and reading, the numbers of failing readers will decrease significantly. Inevitably, though, there will always be pupils who do not respond to this approach and, as a result, fail to acquire fluent written language skills. The effect of this on their subsequent scholastic achievement can be devastating. In this concluding chapter we consider how we can support older students so that they can learn how to get round some of the difficulties.

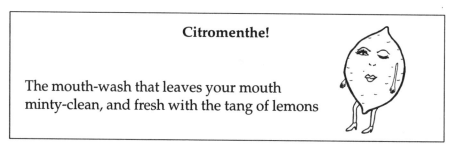

Citromenthe!

The mouth-wash that leaves your mouth minty-clean, and fresh with the tang of lemons

We encounter new words far more frequently than we might imagine. But we rarely stop to consider the complexity of the task which we carry out so effortlessly when new words need to be decoded. Take the name of an hypothetical product. How do you begin to pronounce *citromenthe*?

In the first place you might consider where the syllable boundaries are, and then blend the sounds associated with individual letters within each syllable. This could give /kit//rom//enth/ with the accent on the /rom/. But you probably did not arrive at this pronunciation! It is likely that your pronunciation sounded more like /sit/ /ro/ /menth/ with the stress on the first syllable, /sit/.

Pronunciations of novel words are usually guided by analogies with similar, known words, as well as by specific items of orthographic (spelling) knowledge.

For example, most of us know that when 'c' is followed by 'i' it is pronounced as /s/.

Additionally, our knowledge of what the word means – in this example, a product with specified contents – helps us to confirm the sounds of individual syllables, and also to locate the stressed syllable.

In secondary education, and again in adulthood we encounter new vocabulary which, in many cases, we will also need to be able to read and spell. To do this we call again on the collection of strategies which we've accrued over the years, including alphabetic strategies which in turn rely on phonological skills, and knowledge of spelling conventions – until we have consolidated the words within our spelling- and reading-lexicons.

Reading and writing are usually taught, as curriculum items, only in the first few years of mainstream schooling. Beyond that, it is assumed that the majority of pupils have the literacy skills with which to access an increasingly complex curriculum. But most of us are aware that, while there are some secondary pupils who are weak spellers and slow readers, there is another group of students whose written language skills are so fragile that their access to the curriculum is severely restricted:

- they cannot decode new, subject-specific vocabulary
- they confuse visually-similar words
- their reading is so laboured and effortful that they read less and understand little of what they read
- their writing is characterised by bizarre spellings
- their written expression is immature compared with their oral contributions
- their study skills are poor.

These are the students with severe, complex and persistent difficulties which are sometimes termed **dyslexia**.

For secondary-age students with severe difficulties we need to adopt a change of attitude and a more pragmatic approach to making the most of the skills that they bring to the task. New pressures, linked to approaching examinations which mark the end of compulsory schooling, bear on both student and teacher.

In the secondary years there is very little time left to acquire fluent reading and spelling skills before students embark on external exams and then leave school to meet the literacy demands of adult life.

More spelling rules, for example, or techniques for improving reading rate take second place to helping students to circumvent their difficulties by identifying their own targets and coping mechanisms.

Students without difficulties make use of a range of efficient reading, writing and note-taking strategies which they have developed, usually quite spontaneously through long involvement with literacy and also, casually, from effective teachers. The student whose access to written materials is restricted by very poor reading and writing skills and, as a consequence, who has never fully engaged with learning–teaching situations, does not absorb incidental learning in this way.

Students with complex and persistent literacy difficulties are further disadvantaged by an inability to make use of strategies which depend on intact literacy skills. To compensate, this group will need coping mechanisms. These will emerge from the profiles of strengths and weaknesses which assessment of individual students reveal. Coping mechanisms are most effective when a whole curriculum approach is adopted. Such an approach has the potential:

- to foster a student-centred approach to learning
- to identify coping mechanisms as specific learning targets
- to provide opportunities across the curriculum to apply and support these mechanisms
- to provide a framework for in-service professional development.

A whole curriculum approach: general principles

Schools are places of learning. To provide equality of opportunity the medium through which teaching and learning happen must address the needs of all pupils. In the secondary school, literacy is the predominant medium.

> The student with severe literacy difficulties is seriously disadvantaged, even in topic areas where, given the opportunity to demonstrate knowledge and understanding through an alternative medium, they might excel.

The school needs to be proactive in its management of students with severe, complex and persistent literacy difficulties. Reacting to the specific needs of individuals may compound them if a pupil is isolated. This is particularly true of secondary age pupils who, sensitive to factors affecting peer-approval, are more likely to respond negatively, for example, by resorting to disruptive behaviour, when self-esteem is badly damaged.

A whole-school approach to pupils with severe written language difficulties will recognise that there is a shift of focus in respect of older pupils. For younger pupils, our aim is for them to become competent readers and writers. However, if severe difficulties persist into secondary education we may have to acknowledge that, for these students, fluent and effective literacy may never be attained.

> A study skills approach acknowledges that learners are active participants in their own learning.

A student-centred approach to learning

Young adults who have a long history of difficulties and possibly negative learning experiences need to be aware that their perceptions of their own learning are important and will be taken into account. Involving them in an evaluation of their own strengths and weaknesses and building these into attainable targets gives them new control over their learning, replacing negative defeatism with a more positive outlook.

The practicalities of this entail working with students to set targets, in the form of coping mechanisms which they can practise and apply in all subjects, with teachers and students (and parents, wherever possible) jointly reviewing progress (for example, of Individual Education Plans [DfE, 1994]). According to this view the teacher's role may be one of facilitator, and the pupil takes the responsibility for getting round the demands of the curriculum within a supportive environment.

> Overcoming the difficulties of secondary-age pupils becomes largely a matter of creating and applying coping mechanisms.

The process of generating mechanisms will involve students, in conjunction with all teaching staff, in identifying the aspects of the syllabus which are most affected by their particular difficulties. The next step is to devise and record the mechanisms, as learning targets, in order to compensate for difficulties, and to review them regularly, monitoring their value in terms of pupil and teacher satisfaction.

Coping mechanisms as specific learning targets

> If students are to realise the full potential of the coping mechanisms they have identified they must have the opportunity to apply them in every subject and to have them modelled and reinforced across the curriculum.

Providing opportunities across the curriculum

Students who are struggling with literacy will not spontaneously generalise strategies unless a framework along with clear cues is consistently provided by every subject-teacher.

Fundamental components of an effective whole-school approach are the knowledge and attitudes of all teaching staff. Some INSET provision should be directed towards developing the professional skills which teachers will need to call upon in order to devise, implement and evaluate coping mechanisms alongside their students.

A framework for professional development

Clearly, Special Educational Needs Co-ordinators will want to promote all teachers' knowledge of literacy difficulties and their impact on all learning so that together, they can extend the process of providing this group of students with generalisable strategies for accessing the curriculum.

> A report published in 1992 confirmed that over one-third of the teachers interviewed, all recent graduates, did not believe that issues relating to reading were the concern of secondary school teachers other than staff with responsibilities for students with special needs. Furthermore, many confessed to being unsure about the processes involved in reading (Brooks *et al.*, 1992).

Implementation across the whole curriculum

SENCos and other support staff may often work with affected students in relative isolation. But a whole curriculum approach set up to integrate strategies will be far more effective. Some schools, operating this approach, set out their cross-curricular strategies on Individual Education Plan pro-formas, to be ticked as required for each student. An example, covering a range of written language needs, might be as follows.

Reading skills
- taped texts
- highlighting key words
- scanning for key words

Note-taking skills
- selecting the main idea
- recording key words
- taping part/whole lessons

Spelling skills
- segment words
- copy from a model
- use a spell-check

Subject vocabulary skills
- personal dictionary
- multisensory techniques
- understanding the meaning/ derivation of words

Further differentiation for students with phonological difficulties

Techniques such as these can be used to support all students with weak written language skills. However, we usually find that they need to be fine-tuned to help those with severe and persistent problems, stemming from phonological processing difficulties. The most appropriate blend of strategies will become apparent according to the needs of individual students. Here we suggest some ways in which the modifications suggested above might be interpreted for students who are most severely affected by written language difficulties.

Reading skills

• taped texts

• highlighting key words

•scanning for key words

Taped texts

Students with persistent difficulties will not spontaneously connect unfamiliar words that they hear with written equivalents unless they are guided in their use of this facility. They will find taped texts invaluable (either commercially available 'talking books', or texts which have been specially prepared for the student by a friend, a parent or a Support Assistant). The student should, however, be directed to use tapes, strictly in conjunction with written text, not as an alternative to reading. At the same time, wherever possible, they should highlight difficult words, for example characters' names in fiction, and treat those as key words, analysing them as we suggest in the next section.

Highlight key words

Students are often encouraged to highlight key words. But for the students we are discussing here we need to add extra advice to make the strategy work. Those with severe reading and spelling problems will probably need to identify more words than their peers so **they must have their own copies of important texts**. Additionally, because they rely very heavily on visual patterns, and rarely set up auditory models, they are likely to confuse words of similar appearance, for example, *humidity* and *humidify*; or, *experience* and *experiment*. To counter possible confusion, use different coloured highlighting pens to underline words, and pick out the difference by shading through the syllables or letters which differentiate the two words.

This tendency to confuse words which have very similar orthographic appearances is liable to cause particular problems for these students in examinations, where the stress factor could lead them to make more mistakes than usual. As part of the preparation for examinations students should practise reading the rubric of exam question papers, and noting the format of the questions with particular attention to words such as *compare/contrast*; *describe/discuss*. Where confusable words can be visually differentiated (as in *compare/contrast*) the student can draw around the word to highlight its overall shape.

compare   contrast

Scan for key words

Students with poorly established reading skills tend to assume that if they want to find references to specified topic areas they need to read an entire text. It should be pointed out to them that they can scan the text for specific words, *but*, again, they need to be aware of possible confusions with similar words. Therefore they must keep the sound of the required word firmly in the mind's ear, by sub-vocalising.

Note-taking skills

• selecting the main idea

• recording key words

• taping part/whole lessons

Select the main idea

Pupils with phonological difficulties are often concerned that they won't be able to tackle the spelling of the words representing the main ideas within the subject-topic or piece of work. In addition to the anxiety that this creates, a poor auditory memory (see Chapters 3 and 4, about the links between poor auditory memory and phonological difficulties) make it very difficult for them to listen, remember, select and write. They can be encouraged:

• To develop a system of shorthand that works for *them*.
  For example, writing the numeral '2' instead of *to*, *too* or *two*. The correct version can then be inserted when the student has time to think about it.

• To disregard spelling for note-taking, as long as the writer can understand what has been written.

• To use symbols, pictures, charts, diagrams, numerals, initials to replace whole words or ideas, wherever possible.
  For example, < (less than); NB (emphasis, must); = (the same as ...); + (in addition to; as well as).
  In certain subjects, for example history and science, it is quite appropriate to use diagrams and flow-charts to represent sequential ideas, as an alternative to continuous text; thus the approach can be used routinely with the whole class or teaching-group.

• To write on alternate lines, leaving space to make corrections, and insertions.

As teachers, we can help by preparing students for the main idea:

• summarise what we're going to say, in advance

• summarise what we've said, at the end

- provide a framework for drafting notes
- keep key words on display throughout the lesson.

Record key words

Even though certain words have been repeated and displayed numerous times these students may still forget or confuse them. It is quite likely that some students will also regularly mispronounce words – *persific* for *specific*, for example. In this particular example, the potential for confusion with *Pacific* is obvious, and the likelihood of a correct spelling, remote. The suggestion made in the previous section – that key words should be kept on display throughout the lesson – does not only apply to when the key word is first introduced. Although it seems tedious it is advisable to display some words in every lesson where they are used.

Tape the lesson

Taping lectures is becoming increasingly common in higher education, particularly for students with educational needs. This practice is gradually being taken up in some secondary schools. However, even though part of or all the lesson may be tape-recorded the student will still require notes of essential points. Making notes from a tape may be a good opportunity to practise note-taking skills and consolidate learning, particularly when the pressures are removed. Students may want to ask the subject teacher to check notes for accuracy.

Spelling skills

- copying from a model

- segmenting words

- using a spell-check

Copy words from a model

We know that pupils with poor phonological skills tend not to 'hear' words they have read. That is, they do not set up an inner voice to support their memory. When copying from a whiteboard or OHP they try to carry a complete 'picture'. This, of course, overloads the visual memory, words are misspelt, phrases are omitted. The following techniques might be proposed for these students:
- Say short phrases silently (sub-vocally).
- Regularise the sound of words with irregular spellings, for example, call 'muscle', 'mus/kle' (weak spellers also benefit from this technique!)

- Ask for paper copies of OHPs. Photocopy important pieces of text so that students can add their own mnemonics.
- Syllabify long words. For example: *'re-mem-ber'*, otherwise often spelt as *'rember'*. Copy in chunks, working from the parts to the whole.
- Pronounce deliberately each syllable in words from which sounds can get lost. For example: *'govern/ment'*.

Segment words

Effective readers segment complex words at syllable boundaries, 'automatically'. Individuals with phonologically-based difficulties do not utilise this strategy unless it has been taught and extensively practised. In the previous paragraph it was suggested how syllabification can support copying from models. The same process may help a writer to retrieve spellings, but will require further reinforcement if it is to be totally effective. One possible strategy is to segment a word in terms of meaning, as well as phonological structure:

> *government – we hope a government can govern.*

(Note: don't suggest, *a government governs*, because in that example the sound /n/ again loses its salience.)

Encourage students to refer to the word root or stem when attempting a spelling and when checking spellings. Students need to be reminded that they have a tendency to produce spellings as one 'string' which relies on a vague, visual 'print-out'. Once they realise that there is an alternative to this technique they may find it easier to resist the tendency.

Where a student has the support of a classroom assistant additional techniques can be employed to establish spellings of important but difficult subject words. For example, rebus sums, if tailor-made to the vocabulary needs of individuals, are an enjoyable and effective way of getting students to analyse words.

Rebus sums

These games with words often appear in puzzle books intended for younger children. Students with severe and persistent difficulties may never have attempted them because of their resistance to reading-based activities. They need a lot of preparation to benefit from such games.

> 'To do these puzzles you need to think about the *sounds* of words. Don't worry about the spellings, for the moment. We'll do the first few together ...'

Examples:

retail — 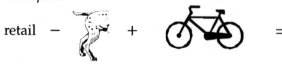 =

This one says, *'retail*, take away *tail*, add on *cycle*, gives *recycle'*.

This one is *'rely*, minus /i/, add /ate/ equals *relate'*.

Rebus sums can also be used to word-build, using pictures, single letters and written syllables. For example:

+ age + + /t/ = management

Examples of other words which have segments that can be graphically represented to feature in rebus sums are:

> government/environment; decrease; belief/relief; defeat;
> defence/offence. Any words ending in -ise; -ble; -ty; -tent;
> -tense/-tence.

Note: the syllables represented by graphics must sound like the word you are representing. Sometimes, although the spelling suggests one pronunciation, the stress patterns produce another. For example, compare *remediate* and *immediate*. For *remediate*, you could represent the final syllable with the figure, '8' but not for *immediate*.

Colleagues may object to rebus sums because they necessarily take liberties with conventional spellings. We argue that an unconventional, but phonologically plausible, spelling is better than an unrecognisable collection of letters.

Linking spelling-patterns with meaning
Many students fail to notice that some words group together because they belong to the same root or base. For example, *chemistry, chemical, chemist*. Students may try to generate a spelling from 'scratch', or if they do recognise a similarity to a known word in the meaning and/or the sound, they don't know where, in the word, they should make the necessary adjustments. Where students have additional support they should perhaps practise charting the developments of polysyllabic, 'family' words.

Wordbuilding activity

Take the word *electric*. Construct it with wooden or plastic letters (*not* brightly-coloured, chunky letters which are clearly intended for pre-schoolers!). Alternatively, personal A4 size whiteboards and coloured markers which give scope for trial-and-error, are becoming very popular with secondary-age students, and so have 'street cred'. Help the student to:
- divide the word into syllables
- locate the vowels

- add to it to make it read *electricity*
- locate the stressed syllables
- discuss the change of sound represented by the 'c'
- break it down again to *electric*
- talk about suffixes, *-al*, *-ly*
- modify it to say *electrical*, *electrically*
- discuss prefixes
- modify *electric* to say/read '*electro-*'
- build *electromagnetic*.

Students should also write each new word generated, either in cursive script or on a word-processor, according to their normal mode of presentation.

It may be necessary to explain the origin of certain spellings, for example, many scientific words are of Greek origin, so scientists have adopted Greek spellings. For example, the /k/ sound is spelt, '*ch*'.

It is also important to tell science students that many scientific words are compounds of meaningful components. That is, use the scientific discipline itself as the approach to dealing with an analysis of its vocabulary. Breaking words down as far as the root, and then rebuilding into a new word is easily and effectively achieved on a word-processor. Remember, the new word must relate to the original word in terms of meaning. Failure to recognise the patterns which relate to sound differences can lead to inaccurate reading, for example: *biological*; *biochemical*.

Otherwise students sometimes adopt **mnemonics** (serious or light-hearted memory-aids) to remember spelling patterns. For example, *there's 'sin' in bu<u>sin</u>ess*. Many students with poor phonological skills compensate by being unusually adept at spotting *visual* patterns.

Note: it is not a good idea to generate long sentences as mnemonics because these often make more demands on memory resources than the original spelling! As a general rule mnemonics that the user invents or chooses are the most useful.

Most of the techniques outlined in this chapter are based on the same fundamental principle which underpins early phonological training: to use language (spoken or written) fully and effectively we need, from time-to-time, to reflect on it as an object of study in its own right. This idea has been illustrated by analogy with glass in windows: we usually use the glass to see the world beyond. Occasionally, we need to look at the glass instead.

Use a Spell-Check

In this book we have made few references to the potential of the word-processor to support students with severe written language difficulties. This is principally because we don't believe that this facility can make any real impact on phonologically-based problems, but it is an excellent tool with which to draft and experiment. We must, though, add a note of caution: the spell-check facility can offer little help when a bizarre spelling is produced. Similarly, it cannot spot a real-word 'near-miss', for example: *personal* instead of *personnel*.

Subject vocabulary skills

• personal dictionary

• multisensory techniques

• understanding the meaning/ derivation of words

People with poor phonological skills have difficulty memorising new words, for example, items in a subject-specific vocabulary. Potential difficulties with pronunciation have already been noted above, and obviously where the spoken version is not fully specified the spelling is likely to be impaired. More significantly perhaps, when learning a new topic the vocabulary or new words become 'pegs' to which accumulating knowledge are attached. Students must be aware of why it is important to adopt subject words, to use them and not to confuse them with other words (e.g. *pollution/pollination*). The same multisensory strategies which are used to establish the spelling of these words will consolidate them in the aural memory.

A personal dictionary
Students should be encouraged to organise their dictionaries in the way which *they* find most helpful (both for recording and for retrieving). Students with severe and persistent difficulties rarely choose an alphabetic arrangement. They might opt to record according to subject area, meaning, word shape, frequency of use or other features which are particularly salient for them.

A major factor in determining the usefulness of the dictionary is the way in which words are recorded and the ease with which the correct words can be retrieved when needed. For example, the words *pollution* and *pollination* could well appear on the same page and in a similar subject area, but could be effectively distinguished by a small flower drawn next to *pollination*.

As an alternative to a book, some students prefer to keep their dictionary in a card-index. This lends some appeal because it appears to be more 'adult'. Additionally, the cards can be re-ordered, according to changing needs, and can be taken out at random to revise spellings or test understanding.

Multisensory techniques

Multisensory strategies are commonly used as teaching techniques. But we can take them a step further. We must actively make clear that these techniques can be developed into a range of coping mechanisms. Each student can then be encouraged to apply consciously the methods they find most helpful. For example:

- tapping out the syllables of a new word while saying it
- identifying a part of the word which has a particular link with the meaning, such as the *'photo'* portion of *photosynthesis* clearly links with the idea of light
- writing out the word and exploring similarities and differences with similar word shapes.

Derivation of words

Reflecting on the derivation of words is interesting as an object of study in itself and can be a helpful way of recalling component parts of long words. Students enjoy this and find it valuable but would almost never find out this information for themselves. Instead subject teachers can incorporate this when introducing new topic words as a class-teaching point, when hopefully it can be developed by more able pupils who will generalise the knowledge to other related words. For example, students who understand the derivation of the prefix, *geo-*, will be well placed to spell a range of related words, and to begin to deduce the meaning of new words such as *geocentric*.

This final chapter has been concerned with suggesting the outlines of techniques which students might develop as coping mechanisms. Teachers and support assistants working within a whole school approach can reinforce and promote their value. Clearly the Special Educational Needs Co-ordinator has a major role in orchestrating the efforts of staff and students; in providing in-service professional training for both teachers and support staff; in advising colleagues on the broad principles of managing students with severe written language difficulties (marking students' work for content rather than presentation, for example); in the review process, and in liaising with parents who are well placed to support their children as they extend some of the strategies outlined here. But, we have emphasised, success will be achieved only if students are fully aware of their own strengths and weaknesses and can develop the study techniques which work best for them.

Throughout this book our message has been that knowledge provides the key to success. As teachers, a thorough understanding of the potency of phonological skills for the acquisition of effective reading–spelling strategies enables us to maximise opportunities for promoting a fundamental skill. Activity-based packs and other ready-made resources have their place as reinforcers of teaching, but their range of application is limited. The most valuable resource lies in a teacher's capacity to discover individual pupil's strategic approaches to acquiring basic skills, and to develop them along lines which will lead to independent learning.

Conclusion

Glossary of Terms

alphabetic	referring to the system whereby written-down letters represent phonemes
analogy	a technique in which a parallel is drawn between something familiar and something not yet known, in an attempt to understand the new item
cognitive	referring to intellectual processes
decoding	assembling a pronunciation of a word from written-down letters
encoding	producing a written form for a spoken word
grapheme	a letter or a group of letters representing a single speech sound
lexicon	an individual's word-bank or 'dictionary-in-the-head'
linguistic	referring to language
logographic	referring to a system in which single pictures or symbols represent whole words
mnemonics	memory-aids, or memory-tricks
onset	the portion of the syllable which precedes the vowel
orthography	a spelling-system
phoneme	the smallest unit of sound which can change the meaning of a word
phonics	usually taken to mean an understanding of the correspondence between speech sounds (phonemes) and letters (graphemes)
phonological awareness	an explicit awareness of the segmental nature of spoken language
phonology	relating to the speech sound system

rhyme a short verse; the correspondence between two words which share the same rime

rime the portion of a syllable which includes the vowel and any final sounds

syllable a unit of sound or sounds which are pronounced together as a single beat

working memory a component of short-term memory which temporarily holds information while the individual carries out some intellectual task

Bibliography

Adams, M. J. (1994) *Beginning to Read: Thinking and Learning about Print.* Cambridge, Mass.: MIT Press.

Alegria, J. and Morais, J. (1991) 'Segmental analysis and reading acquisition'. In Rieben, L. and Perfetti, C. (eds) *Learning to Read: Basic Research and its Implications.* Hillsdale, NJ: Lawrence Erlbaum Associates.

Blachman, B. (1991) 'Early intervention for children's reading problems: Clinical applications of the research in phonological awareness', *Topics in Language Disorders*, **12[i]**, 51–65.

Brooks, G., Gorman, T., Kendall, L. and Tate, A. (1992) *What Teachers in Training are Taught about Reading: The Working Papers.* Slough: NFER.

Broomfield, H. and Combley, M. (1997) *Overcoming Dyslexia: A Practical Handbook for the Classroom.* London: Whurr Publishers.

Bryant, P. E. and Bradley, L. (1985) *Children's Reading Problems.* Oxford: Basil Blackwell.

Department for Education (1994) *Code of Practice on the Identification and Assessment of Special Educational Needs.* London: Central Office of Information.

Ehri, L. (1987) 'Learning to read and spell words', *Journal of Reading Behaviour*, **19**, 5–31.

Ellis, A. (1984) *Reading, Writing and Dyslexia: A Cognitive Analysis.* London: Lawrence Erlbaum Associates.

Frith, U. (1985) 'Beneath the surface of developmental dyslexia'. In Patterson, K., Coltheart, M. and Marshall, J. (eds) *Surface Dyslexia.* London: Lawrence Erlbaum Associates.

Fudge, E. C. (1969) 'Syllables', *Journal of Linguistics*, **5**, 253–86.

Gathercole, S. E. and Baddeley, A. D. (1993) *Working Memory and Language.* Hove: Lawrence Erlbaum Associates.

Goswami, U. (1995) 'The role of analogies in reading development'. In Gains, C. and Wray, D. (eds) *Reading Issues and Directions.* Stafford: NASEN.

Goswami, U. (1996a) 'Rhyme and Reading', *Child Education*, April, 16–17.

Goswami, U. (1996b) 'Rhyme and Analogy', *Child Education*, May, 28–9.

Hatcher, P. (1994) *Sound Linkage: An Integrated Programme for Overcoming Reading Difficulties.* London: Whurr Publishers.

James, F. (1996) *Phonological Awareness: Classroom Strategies.* Shepreth: UKRA.

Layton, L. and Deeny, K. (1996) 'Promoting phonological awareness in preschool children'. In Snowling, M. and Stackhouse, J. (eds) *Dyslexia, Speech and Language: A Practitioner's Handbook.* London: Whurr Publishers.

Layton, L., Deeny, K., Upton, G. and Tall, G. (1996) *Phonological Awareness and the Pre-School Child: Final Report to the DfEE*. Birmingham: The University of Birmingham.

Maclean, M., Bryant, P. and Bradley, L. (1987) 'Rhymes, nursery rhymes and reading in early childhood', *Merrill-Palmer Quarterly*, **33[3]**, 255–81.

Marsh, G., Friedman, M. P., Desberg, P. and Saterdahl, K. (1981) 'Comparison of reading and spelling strategies in normal and reading disabled children'. In Friedman, M. P., Das, J. P. and O'Connor, N. (eds) *Intelligence and Learning*. New York: Plenum.

Pinker, S. (1994) *The Language Instinct*. New York: William Morrow and Company.

Reason, R. and Boote, R. (1994) *Helping Children with Reading and Spelling*. London: Routledge.

Spector, J. E. (1992) 'Predicting progress in beginning reading: dynamic assessment of phonemic awareness', *Journal of Educational Psychology*, **84[3]**, 353–63.

Stackhouse, J. (1989) 'Relationship between spoken and written language disorders: Implications in an educational setting'. In Mogford, K. and Sadler, J. (eds) *Child Language Disability*. Clevedon: Multilingual Matters.

Treiman, R. (1985) 'Onsets and rimes as units of spoken syllables', *Journal of Experimental Child Psychology*, **39**, 161–81.

Wilson, J. (1993) *P.A.T. Phonological Awareness Training: A New Approach to Phonics*. London: Educational Psychology Publishing, UCL.

Index